CON

WOW!
DISCOVERIES, INVENTIONS, IDEAS and EVENTS
that Changed the World

Philip Ardagh writes both fiction and non-fiction, and is a familiar face at book festivals in England, Ireland, Scotland and Wales. His books have been translated into numerous languages, including Latin.

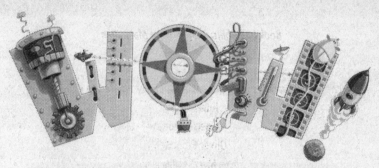

DISCOVERIES, INVENTIONS, IDEAS and EVENTS
that Changed the World

Philip Ardagh

Illustrated by
Sally Kindberg and Mike Phillips

MACMILLAN CHILDREN'S BOOKS

Discoveries, Inventions, Ideas and *Events* all first published 2000 by
Macmillan Children's Books

This edition published 2002 by Macmillan Children's Books
a division of Macmillan Publishers Limited
20 New Wharf Road, London N1 9RR
Basingstoke and Oxford
www.panmacmillan.com

Associated companies throughout the world

ISBN 0 330 40049 5

1 3 5 7 9 8 6 4 2

A CIP catalogue record for this book is available from the British Library.

Typeset by Nigel Hazle
Printed and bound in Great Britain by Mackays of Chatham plc, Kent

DISCOVERIES
that Changed the World

For my parents,
and about time too

DISCOVERIES!

Imagine a world where no one has discovered anaesthetics so, if you need your leg amputated, you'll be wide awake and feeling the pain whilst the surgeon saws through your bone . . . or a world where no one has discovered germs, so we've done nothing to stop them spreading. (You might eat off the same old dirty plate, or never have clean sheets.) Imagine a world where we haven't found a way of working out where we are when we're out at sea, and a world where America hasn't been discovered by Europeans. Think of a world with no electricity, no plastics, no knowledge of the fact that atoms themselves can be changed to create terrifying nuclear explosions. In this *WOW!* book, we take a look at some of these incredible discoveries and how they've altered just about everything around us. As for the future, we can only guess. Who knows what's out there, waiting to be discovered, perhaps by one of YOU?

PHILIP ARDAGH
2000

1

SECRETS OF THE UNIVERSE

FEBRUARY 1633, THE PAPAL COURT, ROME

Galileo Galilei has written a book in which he argues that both Heaven and Earth are governed by the same natural laws and are both part of a solar system which, in turn, is part of an even greater universe. Worse than that, he has argued that the Earth is not the centre of this universe and that the Earth revolves around the sun and does NOT remain stationary whilst the sun revolves around it.

This final (and wholly accurate) claim goes totally against the teachings of the Church. He could be put to death for such **heresy**, so reads out a document saying that he was wrong. When he finishes, there are those who claim that he mutters 'Still it moves' — meaning the Earth around the sun — whatever the Pope and the Holy Catholic Church might think!

HEAVEN AND EARTH

The first true humans were probably too busy looking for food and trying to keep alive to think about big issues such as the shape of the Earth but, once people did take an interest in these matters, they probably assumed that it was well and truly flat. It makes sense, doesn't it? Why should the Earth be any other shape? If it was round, you'd fall off it, wouldn't you? To begin with, people had no idea that the Earth was a planet hanging in space, up there with all the other planets and stars. Why should they? Down here was Earth and up there were the heavens. And that was the end of the story.

NOT THAT FLAT?

Then people must have started to spot clues that the Earth might not be flat after all. The biggest clue of all is the horizon – the line where the land (or the water) appears to join the sky. (The best place to see the horizon is looking out to sea, because there are no hills or trees or buildings in the way.) If you're standing on the quayside watching a ship sailing off out of port and into the distance, whilst your friend is watching the same ship from high in a tower directly above you, you can make two important observations. First, the horizon line between the sea and the sky isn't a straight line. It's slightly curved. Secondly – even if you have equally

good eyesight – your friend will see the ship for longer than you do before it disappears from view. Why? Because the reason why you can't see the ship any more isn't because it's so far away that it's such a tiny dot that you can't see it, but because it's gone *over* the horizon. In other words, it's gone over the curve of the Earth. That's also why the friend in the tower can see the ship for longer. Because they're higher up, they can see further over the curve so are, in fact, seeing a different horizon line to you. And why is the horizon line curved, not straight? Because the world is round, not flat.

BACK IT UP

It's a common **misconception** that, until the days of Christopher Columbus and people like him, everyone assumed that the world was flat and that people might one day sail over the edge. But what about Atlas? Not *an* atlas – not a book of maps – but *the* Atlas, the Ancient Greek god who carried the world on his shoulders. The 'world' was often simply shown as the Earth and the Ancient Greeks represented it as the sphere (round object) it is . . . and that was *thousands* of years ago. Many Ancient Greek astronomers argued that the Earth hung, stock-still, like a globe on an invisible string, whilst all the stars and planets moved around it. But at least they got the shape right.

ON THE BALL

Then an Ancient Greek named Aristarchus of Sàmos came up with an amazing theory: that the Earth turned around on its axis – an invisible line running between the North and South Pole – every twenty-four hours and that it revolved around the sun, along with all the other planets.

4

What was amazing was that, first, Aristarchus came up with this theory over 2,200 years ago; secondly, that few, if anyone, believed him; and, thirdly, that he was right!

GOD'S GRAND DESIGN

Unfortunately for the advance of science, another Ancient Greek called Ptolemy came along about 400 years later – that's still over 1,800 years ago – and produced lots of astrological maps and charts showing a stationary Earth, not the sun, at the centre of things. And it was Ptolemy's view that was believed and taken up by the Christian Church. As far as the Church was concerned, the Universe was God's creation and humans were his 'children'. *Of course* He would have placed them at the very centre of the world.

A DANGEROUS TRUTH

The Polish astronomer Nicolaus Copernicus certainly didn't agree. In 1530, he finished a book packed full of his discoveries and theories. He hadn't known of the much earlier theories of Aristarchus of Sàmos, but had reached the same conclusions, using astrological observation and mathematics: that the Earth turned around once each day as it moved around the sun, as did all the other planets. This is called the 'heliocentric' system, because Helios was the Greek god of the sun and 'centric' means 'centred'. Galileo Galilei (1564–1642) looked through his nice new telescope, agreed with Copernicus, expressed his views, and ended up in the mess we found him at the beginning of this chapter. But, slowly, people began to realize the truth of such claims. Galileo didn't lose his life, but was put under house arrest for his 'crimes'.

STICK TO IT

So here we all are on a round Earth, spinning on its axis between the North and South Poles, and also revolving around the sun but – er – how come we don't fall off? *You* know the answer's an invisible force called gravity, and *I* know that the answer's an invisible force called gravity, but that's only because someone has already discovered the answer for us! That person was Englishman Sir Isaac Newton.

GETTING THE BALL ROLLING

Galileo himself had done experiments on dropping objects, but hadn't stopped to consider *why* things fall in the first place. He was more interested in disproving the popularly held belief that heavy objects fall faster than light ones. In other words, he wanted to disprove the belief that if a heavy object and a light object are dropped at the same time, the heavier object will hit the ground first. The reason why this was so widely believed was because it apparently seemed easy to prove: drop a brick and a feather together and we all know that the brick will hit the ground first. Galileo argued that this had nothing to do with weight. And, once again, he was right. The reason why the feather falls slower has to do with other factors, such as **air resistance**. By rolling solid balls of different weights and sizes down a ramp, and timing their descent, he found that they all took the same length of time to reach the bottom. In other words: drop two solid balls of different weights, and under ideal conditions – without wind resistance – they'd hit the ground at the same time. Roll them down a ramp and they actually do!

An American astronaut was able to put Galileo's theory to the test over 300 years later, by carrying out the experiment on the moon. Because the moon has no atmosphere, there's no air resistance. The astronaut dropped two balls of different weights and size and, with the moon's gravity being far less than Earth's, they fell very slowly to the ground . . . hitting it at the same time. Which brings us neatly back to gravity.

GRAVITY

Whether Isaac Newton really did start thinking about gravity after he got a bonk on the head from an apple falling from a tree, or whether that's just a good story, understanding gravity was certainly a remarkable achievement. He worked out that there is a 'force of attraction' between any two objects (you and the Earth, for example), and that this force is proportional to the total **mass** of these objects (with the enormous Earth's pull on you much greater than your pull on it). Going back to the brick and the feather, the reason why they would fall at the same rate (if there was no air resistance) is because the *total* mass of Earth+brick is almost exactly the same as that of Earth+feather.

THE LAWS OF THE UNIVERSE

Newton also made many other important discoveries and observations. For example, he proved that white light – ordinary sunlight – is made up of the colours of the rainbow (a **spectrum** of different coloured light), that the pull of the moon does indeed control the Earth's tides (something Galileo had suspected). He is also well-known for his three laws of motion, explaining how moving objects behave (even when they run into each other). Newton put together all his discoveries and theories into a book called the *Principia* (1687) which, even today, is still regarded by many to be one of the greatest scientific books ever written. It contained everything from the fact that the Earth didn't orbit the sun in a circle, but an oval (elliptical) orbit, to why pendulums swing the way they do!

SO WHAT?

It's thanks to the dedication, commitment and discoveries of men such as Galileo and Newton that the age of true science was born and that people really began to make sense of the world around them, and realized why things happened in the way they did. Once people could understand the basic principles and natural laws of the workings of the universe, then they could begin to use this knowledge to invent new products and to develop new ideas for the benefit of humankind. Newton's view of the universe – sometimes described as being the 'clockwork mechanics' view – still helps to explain gravity, motion and much of what goes on around us. In the twentieth century, however, German-born Albert Einstein was about to turn some of those Newtonian theories on their heads!

RELATIVITY

14 MARCH 1879, ULM, GERMANY

Pauline has just given birth to her first child. It's a healthy boy and both Pauline and her husband Hermann are delighted. Hermann is an electrical engineer at a time when electrical products are a new and exciting area to work in. Next year, he'll be moving his family to Munich to team up with his brother Jacob to make electrical equipment. Who knows? This newborn baby boy might grow up to be a fine electrical engineer himself, one day. He might even take over the company. They'll call him Albert. That's it: Mr and Mrs Hermann Einstein and their son Albert. Who knows what the future might bring young Albert Einstein?

IT'S ALL RELATIVE

Imagine you're standing at the edge of the road, holding a machine which records the speed of passing objects. If a car is driven past at 60 mph (miles per hour) the machine will, of course, register 60 mph. Now imagine you're in a car being driven at 40 mph, and you stick your machine out of the window at the car driving at 60 mph alongside,

10

what speed will the machine register now? 20 mph, because *relative to the car you're in* (going 40 mph) the car going 60 mph is only going 20 mph faster.

STRAIGHT LIGHT

The speed of light (unlike the speeds of the cars in the imaginary experiment above) is *constant*. In other words, if you're standing still when you point the speed-recording machine at a beam of light or if you're in a rocket car travelling at 600 mph, the speed will always be recorded as 186,000 miles per second. Not miles per hour. Per *second*. (This is an approximate figure; a more accurate one is 299,792,458 metres per second in a **vacuum**.) We know that light always travels in a straight line (at the speed of light) because if it could bend and flow like water, there wouldn't be shadows – which are simply the absence of light. (It would go round corners and everything would be bright!)

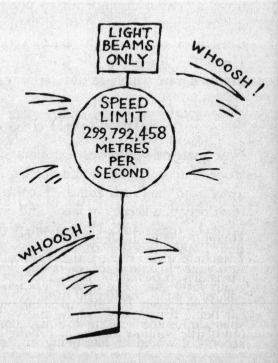

SEEING THE LIGHT!

Albert Einstein, the brilliant scientist who is now everyone's idea of an absolute genius, observed that the acceleration (speeding up) of an object appeared to bend light. But, because he knew that light could only travel in straight lines and *couldn't* be bent, he knew that there must be something else going on. His conclusion was remarkably simple, yet the implications were mind-boggling: light itself wasn't bending, but the time and space through which it was travelling was! This is how he worked it out . . .

SPACE AND TIME

Speed is measured by the time it takes for an object to travel a certain distance (or, to put it more scientifically: distance divided by time). So, if light can only travel at one constant speed through space, yet it appears to bend sometimes, it must be the time and space that have been distorted, and which, in turn, appear to distort light.

THE GRAVITY OF IT ALL!

Now imagine you're an astronaut in a spaceship up in space. You're weightless and floating about because you're away from the Earth and the Earth's gravity. It's the force of gravity that keeps our feet – and everything around us – firmly on the ground. Up in your spaceship, you don't have that. If the spaceship suddenly accelerates, though, you'll find yourself flat on the spaceship floor and – if it's going really fast – the force of acceleration will be so great that you won't even be able to stand up. If, however, your spaceship is accelerating at a nice, constant 9.8 metres per second, it would be like being in a room back on Earth.

The pull of the acceleration would exactly match gravity. Because, under these conditions, gravity and acceleration are the equivalent of each other, this is called the principle of equivalence. So, Albert Einstein argued, if acceleration – of, say, a speeding spaceship – can bend space and time, and gravity behaves like acceleration, then *gravity* can affect space and time too! (And he worked all of this out before there were even such things as spacecraft!) So acceleration behaves like gravity, and gravity attracts objects with less mass to those with greater mass. Einstein reasoned, therefore, that a large object such as the sun would attract something as weightless as light, bending the time and space around it.

A BENDY UNIVERSE

Before Einstein came along and changed everyone's way of thinking, most physicists believed in the science of the universe as put forward by another brilliant person: Sir Isaac (see the Secrets of the Universe chapter). The way Newton saw it, the universe was an ordered place. Einstein realized that it was very different. Imagine a trampoline with a grid of nice straight lines drawn on the flat canvas, representing light travelling in straight lines, at a constant speed, through time and space. Now imagine dropping a large ball in the middle of the trampoline and then another, and then another. When you jump on a trampoline the canvas bends and stretches. It's the same if you drop something heavy on it. These balls will pull down on the canvas of the trampoline, distorting the once-straight lines so that they're all bent and stretched too. The nearer the lines are to a ball, the more wonky they will have become. This was how Einstein saw the universe. The balls were the stars and planets whose gravity – acting like acceleration – were distorting space and time.

BUT WHAT DOES IT MEAN?

The Earth, the sun, the moon and the stars all have gravity of different strengths, so are bending space and time in different ways. And what does this mean? That, up in space, time can go faster or slower relative to time down here on Earth. Why, because if gravity and acceleration can bend time, then 'bent time' will be slower than 'straight time', since – as I've said before – a straight line is the quickest way to get between two points. (So, in theory, an astronaut could come back from the deep reaches of space to find everyone has aged whilst he hasn't – or the other way around!) If you understand this far, then you understand the very basics of Einstein's Theories of Relativity.

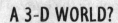

A 3-D WORLD?

We're all aware of living in a three-dimensional world. A very thin line has one basic dimension: length. A square has two basic dimensions: height and width. A real box (as opposed to a drawing of one) has three dimensions: length, width and depth (the front-to-back measurement). If a drawing looks very flat we say it's very two-dimensional. If it looks very lifelike, we say that it looks amazingly three-dimensional. Einstein was thinking in *four* dimensions, an idea first proposed in 1908 by a Russian-German named Hermann Minkowski. That fourth element is space–time: three dimensions in space (as described) and the fourth in time. It is this space–time which is actually bent by gravity and which can only really be shown using mathematical equations.

SUPER SCIENTIST

Einstein became a superstar, although not so much in the scientific world, to begin with, but amongst ordinary people. He went on tours around the world and was greeted by thousands of cheering fans. The only person anywhere near as popular was Charlie Chaplin. Chaplin is supposed to have said that

he was famous because everyone could understand him (in the screen role of a little tramp with a good heart), whereas Einstein was famous because no one could understand him (or his theory, at least)! Many scientists, meanwhile, were reluctant to accept just how brilliant he was. Many didn't think him a 'proper scientist' at first. (When he published his first theory, he was working in the Swiss Patent Office!) The world had to wait a while until some important parts of his theory could be proved. This happened in the 1960s with the first explorations of space.

THE LEGACY

Albert Einstein's Theory of Relativity has turned our understanding of the world on its head. In fact, he published his discoveries and conclusions in two separate papers: *The Special Theory of Relativity* in 1905 and *The General Theory of Relativity* in 1916. (It was in his Special Theory that he included the now infamous equation $E=mc^2$, where E is energy, m is mass and c^2 – c squared – is the speed of light multiplied by itself.) His work not only proved that some of Newton's Laws (the very foundation on which much of modern science was built) were wrong, but also suggested that – in theory at least – time travel, of sorts, is possible. He even got scientists seriously thinking in the fourth – space–time – dimension! Many are still trying to work out all the implications of these amazing scientific discoveries.

THE POWER OF THE ATOM

6 AUGUST 1945, HIROSHIMA, JAPAN

On the orders of the Supreme Allied Headquarters, in a bid to hasten the end of the Second World War in which over 25 million people will have lost their lives, the world's first atomic bomb is dropped on the city by the crew of the *Enola Gay* of the United States Airforce, with the energy of up to 15 kilotons of TNT. President Harry S. Truman of the USA announces, 'We won the race of discovery against the Germans. We have used it to shorten the agony of war.' Reports will later state that 129,558 Japanese men, women and children were killed, injured or missing, their city flattened, and nearly 176,000 survivors were made homeless. Later, tens of thousands will die of radiation burns and sickness. The theory of the awesome, destructive power of the atom has become an explosive fact.

CHOP! CHOP!

Long, long ago in Ancient Greece there were the first real professional thinkers – called philosophers – and one thing a number of them put their minds to was chopping things up. They didn't *actually* chop anything up, you understand. They just thought about it. After all, that was their job. Some argued that, **in theory**, you could go on chopping something up into smaller and smaller pieces for ever. In other words, if humans had brilliant eyesight and small enough, sharp enough, tools, you would *never* reach a stage where something was too small to be cut up further.

17

Other philosophers disagreed. They argued that you must reach a point when you couldn't cut something up any more.

TINY PARTICLES

If that was the case, they argued, what you were left with – these smallest particles that couldn't be cut any smaller – must be the very particles that went together to make up the object. The earliest record of this theory dates all the way back to *c.*400BC (about 2,400 years ago) to two philosophers named Democritus and Leucippus. They thought that these tiny particles probably came in different shapes. (Perhaps, for example, spicy food particles were spiky, which is why they pricked your tongue?) Although the idea was taken up by a later Ancient Greek philosopher, Epicurus, it wasn't until over 2,200 years later that someone gave a name to those tiny particles and developed a fully fledged idea about them. That person's name was John Dalton, and the name he gave the particles was 'atoms'.

THE EXTRAORDINARY MR DALTON

John Dalton was an unusual man. A **colour-blind** English Quaker son of a weaver, he became a teacher at the age of twelve and remained one, in one form or another, for the rest of his life. From 1787, he kept a written record of the weather almost every single day up until he died in 1844 (some 200,000 observations and 57

years later)! It was in 1807 that Dalton published his Atomic Theory, the main ideas of which were:

- All matter is made up of tiny particles, which he named atoms (from the Greek 'atomos', meaning 'that which cannot be divided').
- Atoms cannot be made, divided or destroyed.
- Atoms of the same **element** are identical.
- Chemical reactions are a result of atoms rearranging themselves.
- In **compounds**, atoms can join together to make larger particles.

Dalton later revised his original theory to suggest that an atom *could*, in theory at least, be split into even smaller particles – in other words, that atoms were themselves made up of what we now call **subatomic particles**. He was right. His only real mistake was the belief that all atoms in an element were the same – but that didn't stop his Atomic Theory being mind-blowingly brilliant and changing the way scientists thought about how everything in the universe was made.

19

MODEL MANIA!

Over the next 100 years or so, a number of scientists produced a number of different models to show how they imagined an atom was made up. British scientist J. J. Thomson came up with the 'plum-pudding' model, which looked like an old-fashioned round, Christmas pud (hence the name) but, instead of fruit, it was embedded with representations of negatively charged subatomic grains. It was Thomson who actually went beyond theory to practice, and discovered both negatively and positively charged particles using a piece of equipment called a cathode ray tube (more advanced versions of these are now used in the screen in television sets). New Zealand-born Ernest Rutherford's model had these negatively charged particles (which he called electrons) circling a positively charged **nucleus** at the centre. Danish scientist Neils Bohr went on to improve on Rutherford's model, however, as did James Chadwick, in 1932, with the nucleus in his model made up of positively charged protons and also the neutral (neither positively nor negatively charged) neutrons, which he'd discovered.

AN IDEA OF SIZE

When reading (or writing) about atoms, it's important to remember just how teeny-weenie they really are. They are small divided by small – then even smaller still. Imagine a grain of sand in the palm of your hand or, if you live near a beach like I do, why not actually put a grain of sand in your hand. Now, that's small, isn't it? Yup, but it's made up of thousands of even smaller atoms. In fact, if each of the atoms in that grain of sand grew to the size of that itsby-bitsy, teeny-weenie grain of sand, the grain of sand itself would suddenly be almost 10 km (6.21 miles) wide, and your hand would be s-q-u-a-s-h-e-d. *That's* an idea of just how small the heroes of this chapter are!

THE HEART OF THE ATOM

Now I can tell you that an atom's nucleus is 10,000 times smaller still! And even more incredible, the nucleus itself is made up of even smaller particles! No two elements contain the same number of protons (those positively charged subatomic particles) in their nuclei. This means that an element can be identified by counting the number of protons in the nucleus. This number is called the element's atomic number. Its atomic mass (also a number) is made up of the number of protons in an atom's nucleus – its atomic number – *plus* the number of neutrons.

RADIOACTIVITY

The bigger an atom, the more likely it is to break up. Any atom with an atomic number above 83 has *so many* protons in its nucleus that it becomes unstable and begins to come apart. As it falls to pieces, it becomes radioactive, giving off one of three different types of radiation: alpha, beta or gamma. It was the French scientist Henri Becquerel who discovered radioactivity in 1896, but he didn't know what it was, or even call it that. It is thanks to Polish scientist Marie Curie, and her French husband Pierre, that so much was learnt about it so quickly. Marie discovered two radioactive elements. The first she called polonium, after Poland. The second she named radium. It was even she and Pierre who came up with the term 'radioactivity'. Sadly, Pierre Curie was killed by a cart when crossing the road, but not before he and Marie had won the **Nobel Prize** for Physics in 1903. Marie went on to win the Nobel Prize for Chemistry in 1911. Their daughter, Irène, also became a scientist working on radioactivity. She too won a Nobel Prize in 1935, the year after her mother died.

FISSION

There are two ways of starting a nuclear reaction (the process of creating radiation) and freeing the atom's incredible power. The first is called fission. This was discovered by the German Otto Hahn and Austrian Lise Meitner in the 1930s. They began by working together but, following the rise of **Nazism**, Meitner fled to Sweden to avoid persecution, because she'd been classified Jewish. Hahn sent Meitner the results of his latest experiments on radiation and she showed them to her nephew, another 'Otto', this time Otto Frisch. This collaboration resulted in Hahn revealing the discovery of fission to the world in 1938; that when neutrons were fired at a nucleus, causing it to break into at least two parts, incredible energy was released. By 1942, Italian-born Enrico Fermi had built a nuclear reactor in Chicago, generating electricity with fission. It was the first in the world. (In fact, Fermi had actually achieved fission in 1934, but no one accepted what it was until Hahn's paper was published!)

A-BOMB

Following the outbreak of the Second World War, the now world-famous Albert Einstein – who was, by then, working in the USA – was very worried that the Germans might discover a way of using nuclear fission to make a new type of bomb. The solution, he argued – with a group of other scientists – was to develop an A-bomb (atom bomb) first and wrote a letter to the US President saying so. As a result of this and other pressures, the US Government set up the Manhattan Project in 1943, but Einstein played no part in it. Many other scientists, including Lise Meitner, refused to work on the project. They believed that the destruction caused by the A-bomb would be too great. The director of the Manhattan Project, at Los Alamos, New Mexico, was Robert J. Oppenheimer. Following the dropping of the bomb on the Japanese city of Hiroshima on 5 August 1945 (Germany, Japan's ally, had already surrendered), another A-bomb was dropped on Nagasaki on 9 August. By 14

August, the Japanese had surrendered and the war was over. Many Japanese people who survived the blasts died of radiation burns and sickness, the result of **nuclear fallout**.

FUSION

Even before the bombs were dropped, scientists realized that there was, in theory at least, another kind of nuclear reaction: nuclear fusion. This was where two nuclei are forced together to create one big one. By the end of the war, US and **Soviet** scientists were working on a bomb, **independently**, combining both types of reaction: the fission-fusion bomb. Also called the H-bomb, or thermonuclear bomb, this contained an A-bomb surrounded by a substance containing hydrogen. When the A-bomb was exploded by fission, it would cause the hydrogen nuclei to fuse together to create a second, far greater, fusion reaction. Both the USA and the Soviet Union carried out controlled explosions with H-bombs in the early 1950s. Since then, more and more complicated nuclear weapons have been created, including **intercontinental ballistic missiles**. So far, fortunately, thermonuclear weapons haven't actually been fired or dropped in a real war.

AND THEN?

Today, there are roughly 350 nuclear power stations, supplying about 20 per cent of the world's energy using nuclear fission. This uses a fourth type of radiation – remember alpha, beta and gamma back on page 22 – called neutron radiation. Radiation is also used to treat cancer. Radiation treatment changes the subatomic particles in cancerous cells, making them harmless. A dose of gamma radiation can make most types of food stay 'fresher' longer too. This is called irradiation. An irradiated peach, for example, will still look fresh two weeks after an untreated peach has gone mouldy. There are many people who are not only against nuclear weapons, but *all* human uses of radioactivity. They argue that the possible dangers far outweigh the benefits of unleashing the power of the atom. What's certainly true is that, even if nuclear weapons are never fired in anger and are simply used as a deterrent or a threat, a world with nuclear weapons is a very different place to how it was before.

ELECTRICITY

Astronaut John Glenn is nearing the completion of his Project Mercury Gemini mission and has become the first American to orbit the Earth in space. He will orbit the planet three times in just under five hours and cover about 81,000 miles. As he passes over Australia, he is greeted with the twinkling of thousand upon thousand of lightbulbs as towns and cities light their streetlamps and house lights to send him their good wishes — using the power of electricity.

AMBER

It was those brainy Ancient Greeks — yup, them again — who noticed that if you rubbed a piece of amber, that little pieces of material would become attracted to it and even stick to it. One of the first was probably Thales of Miletus in *c*.600BC. Amber looks like a transparent gem but is, in fact, fossilized tree **sap**. You can tell it was once a liquid because you can often see insects in pieces of amber, trapped when it was still a gooey liquid. (And its colour?

Why, amber of course. No prizes for guessing where the name for *that* colour came from.) What the Ancient Greeks had discovered when rubbing amber was what we now call static electricity.

SHOCKINGLY STATIC

Static electricity doesn't just happen with amber. Rub a balloon on your hair and it will stick to the ceiling. That's another example of static electricity. Occasionally you might go to hold someone's hand – don't go all soppy here – and see a spark pass between you, or feel a little 'shock', especially if you're walking on a nylon carpet. That's yet another example of static electricity. You can also sometimes build up static electricity when stroking a cat, particularly if it's a long-haired one like my cat, Beany. The word 'electric' was invented by an English doctor named William Gilbert in 1600. He chose it because it came from the Greek word 'elektron' meaning . . . guess. Go on, guess. It was Greek for amber. William Gilbert, an Englishman, was very interested in electrical and magnetic **phenomena**.

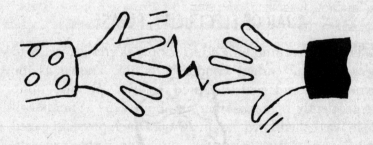

CHARGE!

The first machine especially designed to produce an electric charge – a generator – was described in 1672 in the writings of a German physicist called Otto von Guericke, but it was the Frenchman Charles François de Cisternay Du Fay who made the big breakthrough. He discovered that there were two, clearly different types of electrical charge: positive charges (+) and negative charges (–).

SO WHAT IS ELECTRICITY?

Electricity is, in fact, a form of energy caused by the moving of positively and negatively charged subatomic particles. With electrical charges, dissimilar charges (such as + – or – +) attract each other – as with the amber attracting the pieces of material, or the balloon being attracted to the ceiling and sticking to it – and similar charges (such as + + or – –) repel each other, pushing each other apart. This is usually stated as: 'Like charges repel. Unlike charges attract.' Electricity can be made to flow down a wire, for example, because the charged particles are being attracted to an opposite charge – it's pulling them along, creating an electric current.

A JAR OF ELECTRICITY, PLEASE

A condenser is something which stores electricity, ready to release it. The earliest condenser is now known as the Leyden Jar and was invented by two people, quite independently of each other, in about 1754 – neither of whom was called Leyden. One was a Dutch physicist called Pieter van Musschenbroek and the other was a Pomeranian called Georg von Kleist. Pieter van

Musschenbroek worked at the University of *Leyden* and Ewald, which is where the 'Leyden' name comes from. The original Leyden jar was a glass jar filled with water. In the neck of the jar was a stopper with a nail (or possibly a wire) sticking through both ends, the bottom part in the water. The jar could be charged with electricity by holding the nail sticking from the top of the stopper to a generator – something which generates (or makes) electricity. Once moved from the electrical source, the jar was now stored with electricity. How could you tell? By holding the jar in one hand and touching the nail coming through the top of the stopper with the other – the electricity in the jar was then discharged through your arm, giving you a nasty shock! Your body was acting as a **conductor**, and I don't mean the types you might find in an orchestra or selling you a ticket on a bus.

LIGHTNING

The multi-talented American Benjamin Franklin – scientist, publisher, author and statesperson – was fascinated by electricity. He wanted to prove that atmospheric electricity (in other words thunder and lightning) was the same kind of electricity as a static electric charge. In 1747, he came up with an experiment involving a kite which might help to prove it and this was published in London. As a result, it was successfully carried out in both England and France before he actually put it to the test himself, in the USA, in 1752. This involved flying a kite in a thunderstorm with a metal key tied to the wet string. The lightning hit the string and the electric charge flowed down towards Franklin. (Some people were later killed trying this experiment, **SO DON'T EVEN THINK ABOUT GIVING IT A GO YOURSELF**!!) He then invented

29

the lightning rod (also known as a lightning conductor) for tall buildings. Attached to tall buildings, these rods create a **low-resistance** path for the lightning – so the electric charge runs down the rod to the ground rather than damaging the buildings. For this, and other works, he not only received honorary degrees from the University of St Andrews and the University of Oxford, but also became a fellow of the Royal Society of London and, in 1753, was awarded the Society's very shiny and very important 'Copley Medal'. (Franklin developed a theory that electricity was a 'fluid' that existed in all matter which we now, of course, know is wrong. But, hey, we can't all be right all of the time.)

VOLTS AND AMPS

Another man greatly interested in 'atmospheric electricity' was the Italian physicist Alessandro Volta (1745–1827). He also invented what became known as the Voltaic Pile (c.1800), which produced a source of electricity. It was really the first efficient **battery**. The Emperor Napoleon (boss of France and of 'Not tonight, Josephine' fame) was so impressed with Volta's work that he made him a Count. The electrical unit the **volt** – as in 'DANGER 30,000

VOLTS' – was also named after him in his honour. Another electrical unit, the **amp**, was named after Frenchman André Ampère. He worked on the connection between electricity and magnetism: electromagnetism. Amongst his many impressive discoveries, one involved experiments with two conductors lined up parallel to each other, with electricity passed through them. When an electrical current was passed through the conductors in the same direction, the conductors attracted each other – in other words, they pulled towards each other. But if the electrical currents were passed in the opposite direction, the conductors repelled each other – pushed each other further apart. (The **watt**, by the way,

as in 60-watt lightbulb, was named after the Scottish engineer James Watt, whom you can read about in the next part of this book. In fact, he had little to do with electricity, except that it can be generated using steam power.)

FARADAY'S FIELD DAY

Yet another electrical unit is called the **farad**, and is named after the British scientist Michael Faraday (1791–1867), but isn't so commonly used as volt, amp or watt. Faraday was the son of a blacksmith and didn't get much of an education. He could, however, read and this came in very handy when he became an apprentice to a London bookbinder. As well as binding the books, he managed to read a number of the scientific ones, and they captured his imagination. He was soon conducting experiments of his own in his spare time. His early interest was in chemistry and he was eventually taken on as an assistant to a well-respected scientist called Sir Humphry Davy. He got the job by attending one of Sir Humphry's lectures and sending him some of his notes afterwards. Sir Humphry was mightily impressed, and Faraday ended up going on a European tour with him in 1813. It was Faraday's experiments with electromagnetism in the 1820s and 30s that were his greatest triumph. Amongst other things (and he did make many important discoveries), he discovered that if a wire is passed through a magnetic field – the area affected by a magnet – an electric current passes down that wire. This phenomenon is called 'electromagnetic induction'. The reason why it's such a big deal is because it ultimately led to the invention of the huge electricity generators which are the source of the electricity used to light, heat and power our homes.

LET THERE BE LIGHT

That's the thing about electricity. Once so much was found out about it, once it was *understood*, it could be used to heat, light and power whole cities and to change the world beyond recognition. In the past, people'd had to rely on candles and oil lamps for light and wood, and coal and coke fires for warmth. Then came gas lighting, in the streets and in the home, along with gas fires for warmth. The gas was piped into houses. It was poisonous so, if it leaked, it could either poison you or cause an explosion and blow up you *and* your home! It needed to be lit with a naked flame to give off light and warmth, so was potentially dangerous in that way too. Electricity changed all that. To begin with, a few 'important' buildings had arc lights, where an arc of electricity sparked between two pieces of carbon. These were more for show than any great practical use. They were incredibly bright but burnt out very quickly and didn't cast light over a very big area. Then came the lightbulb.

A BRIGHT IDEA

The lightbulb was invented by Englishman Joseph Swan in 1878, after twenty years' hard work, and – a little later – by inventor and invention-developer, American Thomas Edison (who patented over 1,000 inventions and also appears in *WOW! Inventions that Changed the World*). Although Swan got there first, Edison accused Swan of stealing HIS idea! A legal wrangle followed and, eventually, the two men

formed the Edison and Swan Electric Company. (Swan may have invented the bulb first, but Edison was the more famous, so he made sure that, at least, his *name* came before Swan's!) On New Year's Eve 1879, the streets and houses of Menlo Park – the village where Edison had his laboratories – were lit with electric light. By September 1881, Edison (and the world)'s first electricity power station opened in Pearl Street, New York.

A SHINING BEACON

Today, electricity is one of the most important tools to humankind, and not just for heating, lighting and cooking. Electric fences keep livestock in their fields. Electricity powers the computer I'm typing these words on right now. It powers the alarms which protect property, the traffic lights which control the flow of cars, and everything from telephones and the internet to aeroplanes' flight systems and the radar machines that track them in the sky. Look around you. Discovering the power of electricity and harnessing that power has changed the face of the world. Astronaut John Glenn can testify to that. He saw it with his own eyes from space.

THE NEW WORLD

By proclamation of Benjamin Harrison, the 23rd President of the United States of America, the first pledge of allegiance to the flag is proclaimed in schools throughout the land. The wording of the pledge, which will later be slightly revised, is: 'I pledge allegiance to my flag and to the republic for which it stands: one nation, indivisible, with liberty and justice for all.' And the reason for choosing this date to first state the pledge? It's Columbus Day, in memory of Christopher Columbus, the man who discovered America four hundred years previously, in 1492. But, of course, he didn't really discover North America. Did he?

LAND OF OPPORTUNITY

Not all discoveries that changed the world were scientific. The discovery by Europeans of the Americas – north and south – has made a huge impact on history and the world as we know it. Known by explorers and settlers as the New World, the Americas were only new to them, of course. To the people who

already lived there, they didn't need to be 'discovered'. It was home to them and their ancestors for at least 20,000 years! The sheer size, riches and opportunities offered by the New World made it irresistible to those who found it.

CHRISTOPHER COLUMBUS

For a long, long time, Christopher Columbus was famous for being the first European to discover North America. Then he became famous for being the man who *wasn't* really the first European to discover America, but whom people often *thought* was. So how did all this confusion come about? Christopher Columbus's real name wasn't really Christopher Columbus, for starters. It was Cristoforo Colombo. He was born in the independent city of Genoa, so would be what we now think of as Italian. He got the money for his famous expeditions from Spain, however. His **patron** was Queen Isabella of Castile. Columbus was looking for a quick route to Asia but, in 1492, ended up in the Bahamas, landing on a number of islands which we now call San Salvador, Cuba, the Dominican Republic and Haiti – but *he* still assumed that he was in Asian seas.

SOME SERIOUS CONFUSION

The nearest Columbus actually came to setting foot on North American soil was a year later when, in 1493, he stopped off at Puerto Rico (which, today, is officially part of the USA), after which he set up a colony called Isabella near what is now named Cape Isabella, in the Dominican Republic. He did 'discover' mainland South America, though, when his third voyage took him to Venezuela and the mouth of the mighty Orinoco River. To begin with, Columbus had been given a friendly greeting by the indigenous peoples ('natives') wherever he went. But they soon discovered that these European visitors weren't visitors at all, but were intending to stay and were often harsh and cruel. When Columbus kidnapped large numbers of natives in 1495 and sent them to Spain to be sold as slaves, Queen Isabella sent them back, ordering they be released!

THE CABOT CONNECTION

Probably the first European of that era to step onto genuine North American ground – in what is now Canada and not the USA – was John Cabot, who set sail from Bristol in England in 1497. He even sailed along the New England coast. Before any English readers leap up and down shouting 'YES! Ya boo sucks to you, Columbus!', I should quickly add that Cabot's real name was Giovanni Caboto and, like Columbus, he was born in what is now Italy. He, however, led an *English* expedition and his discovery was what later led to Britain claiming North America as a British colony.

SOUTH AMERICAN RICHES

Following the European discovery of the New World, there were numerous Spanish expeditions and conquests from 1500 onwards, mainly centred on South America (which is why so many languages in the region today are variations on Spanish). One of the most famous **conquistadors** was Hernando Cortés, who destroyed the Aztecs in Mexico. The Aztecs had never seen people on horses and were amazed by the Spanish soldiers but, unknown to either side, an even greater threat was the diseases the conquistadors brought with them. The Aztecs had no immunity to foreign diseases and thousands and thousands died from smallpox and other ailments. Cortés and others weren't only interested in claiming land for their sovereign and power for themselves, though. They'd discovered that South America was rich with gold treasure, and there were rumours of much more.

UNSETTLED SETTLERS

The French and the English, meanwhile, centred most of their efforts on exploring North America. Englishman Sir Walter Raleigh and the very first English **colonists** set off for North America in 1585 and settled on Roanoke Island, off the coast of what is now North Carolina. Like the Spanish in South America, they seemed more interested in finding gold than settling down and creating a new community. Raleigh's second batch of colonists set off in 1857 and also settled on Roanoke Island, which he now named Virginia, after his **sovereign**, Elizabeth I, the Virgin Queen – and it shouldn't be confused with any later US states of that name. The colony was governed by map-maker John White, whose daughter Ellinor was married to one of his staff, Ananias Dare. Ellinor gave birth to a little girl on 18 August 1587. They called her Virginia, after the colony, and she was the very first person of English parents to be born in North America. John White returned to England for supplies. He didn't come back to Virginia Island until 1590 – to find himself in the heart of one of America's greatest mysteries, still unsolved to this day. All the colonists had disappeared and they were never found. The island is now in an area called Dare County, in memory of little Virginia Dare.

HERE TO STAY

The first permanent, successful English colony to be set up in North America was in Jamestown (now in the state of Virginia) on 14th May 1607. Though named after King James I, who succeeded to the throne of England after the death of childless Queen Elizabeth, Jamestown was run by the Virginia Company of London (rather than being an official English royal province). In the beginning, it was a disaster. Thousands of colonists died of disease and starvation and in fights with the native North Americans! Finally, in 1624, the English crown took control of the colony.

SLAVERY

One of the 'great' discoveries in the New World was tobacco, and the demand for it in Europe was so great that more and huge plantations sprang up in North America. So many people were needed to pick the tobacco that, by the end of the seventeenth century, English colonists were importing huge numbers of black slaves from Africa – ancestors of many of today's African Americans. The North American slave trade was born. (You can find out more about the rise and fall of the slave trade in the *Events* part of this book.)

THE FRIENDLY FRENCH

The French, meanwhile, had set up much smaller, better-organized colonies, whose colonists, on the whole, got on far better with the local people, trading furs. They founded Quebec in Canada and controlled areas around the St Lawrence and Mississippi Rivers. The state of Louisiana was colonized by them in the early eighteenth century and was originally named Louisiane after King Louis XIV by the French explorer René-Robert Cavelier, sieur (lord) de La Salle, in 1682.

THE DUTCH EAST INDIA COMPANY

The Dutch, meanwhile, based their claim to certain North American territory on discoveries made by an Englishman on their behalf. Though English, Henry Hudson worked for the Dutch East India Company. In 1609, he sailed into what is now New York Bay and explored the river that is now called the Hudson after him. In 1625, the Dutch set up a colony called New Amsterdam, after the old Amsterdam in the Netherlands. Today, it's better known as New York, after the old York in England!

THOSE PILGRIM PARENTS

Probably the most famous of all the settlers in the New World were those who became known as the Pilgrim Fathers (though there were plenty of mothers and mothers-to-be too, so Pilgrim Parents would be more accurate). These were **low church** Puritans from England, who were being given a very tough time by King Charles I (who later got his head chopped off). In the end, a group of Puritans decided that enough was enough and, on 16 September 1620, 102 of them set sail from Plymouth in their ship the *Mayflower*. They reached North America on 21 November 1620, passing Cape Cod and dropping anchor at what later became Provincetown, Massachusetts. Still on board, 41 of the adult male passengers signed the 'Mayflower Compact' – a set of rules to live by which was, in fact, the first written American **constitution**. Today, there's a big monument there to commemorate this piece of history, but this wasn't where they settled. After searching for the best spot, they upped anchor, landed near the tip of Cape Cod and founded Plymouth Colony on 21 December.

A WHOLE NEW WORLD

So how did the discovery of the Americas by Europeans change the world? Beyond recognition. England's grip over its North American colonies grew tighter and tighter until the American War of Independence (1775–83) led to part of North America breaking free and the formation of the United States of America. Then came the get-rich-quick gold rush of 1848/9, then – from 1861–65 – the American Civil War and, later, the USA's involvement in the First and Second World Wars and its emergence as a world superpower. Now *the* superpower. (You can also read about these wars in the *Events* part of this book.) The descendants of these European settlers, and those who have emigrated to the USA since, make up the population of the most powerful and influential country the world has ever known.

THE TRUE DISCOVERERS?

But, if not Columbus or Cabot, who was the first European to discover the New World? Amazingly, the answer probably goes back over a thousand years to a trader from Iceland called Bjarni Herjólfsson who, in 986, reported seeing what was probably the coastline of the American continent. The honour of being the first Europeans to actually set foot in America should probably go to the Vikings. Leif Ericson – son of the famous Viking Eric the Red – reported he'd visited a place he called

'Wineland' somewhere between what we now call Labrador and New England. Archaeological evidence in Newfoundland suggests this was a strong possibility. The Vikings had discovered the New World nearly 500 years before Columbus or Cabot came close. Which means that it wasn't really such a 'new' New World, after all!

LONGITUDE

William Harrison gingerly opens the padded box containing his father John's timepiece, which has sailed with him all the way from England. If it can be proved that this maritime chronometer – which looks more like a giant fob watch than anything else – has kept accurate time, despite the movement of the ship, the damp air and changes in temperature, it will not only mean that, for the first time in history, sailors will be able to chart their exact position at sea with accuracy, but also that William's father John will be eligible for a fortune in prize money! Any more than 2 minutes out, and the prize is lost . . .

GRID LINES

If you look at a modern globe, you'll see that the Earth has been divided up by a grid of lines. There are parallel lines, running horizontally east to west. These are called lines of latitude. Then there are lines running vertically from North to South, *not* parallel, and all of them cutting through both North and South Poles. These are called lines of longitude. The words 'latitude' and 'longitude' come from the Latin *latus*, meaning wide and *longus*, meaning length.

0° LATITUDE AND 0° LONGITUDE

The line of latitude running around the 'middle' of the Earth (like a belt) is called the Equator and is described as

0° latitude. Anywhere below the Equator is described as being in the southern hemisphere. Anywhere above it is in the northern hemisphere. The middle line of longitude is called the prime meridian and is described as 0°. Dividing up maps with grid lines is a very, very, *very* old idea indeed, by the way. An Ancient Greek named Eratosthenes was drawing maps with grid lines over 2,000 years ago!

MAP REFERENCES

To indicate a place on the globe you can give a map reference, stating the square in the grid where it will be found. To be even more accurate, each degree of latitude and longitude can be divided into 60 smaller units called minutes which, in turn, are divided into 60 seconds. (Each minute is one sea mile in length.) This way, anywhere in the world can be pinpointed. For example, the city of Edinburgh in Scotland can be found at 55° 55' N latitude, 3° 11' W longitude.

THE PROBLEM OF LONGITUDE

In the past, although most countries used lines of latitude and longitude on their maps, they didn't all agree which the prime meridian 0° line of longitude should be. They wanted it running through *their* particular country. (The matter was finally decided in 1884, when it was agreed that the line should run directly through Greenwich in London.) A far bigger problem was how to work out what your longitude was when you were at sea. Latitude could be worked out easily enough, using a special measuring instrument called a sextant, but longitude couldn't, which was a real problem for even the most experienced sailors.

Half a map reference isn't much help when you're trying to plot your position out of sight of land!

A MATTER OF TIME

The Earth revolves a full 360° in 24 hours, which means that it must be revolving at a rate of 15° per hour. (I came up with that number simply by dividing 360 by 24.) For every 15° you travel east, the local time moves forward one hour, so every degree of longitude represents 4 minutes of time. If you know what time it is in Greenwich (at 0° longitude) and what time it is where you are, local time (from the position of the sun in the sky), then you can work out your longitude. How? By multiplying the difference between the times by 15 (because one hour equals 15°, remember). For example, if you're travelling east and it's 12:00 midday local time on board ship and still only 8:00 am back in Greenwich, then the difference is 4 hours.

Now, multiply that difference by 15° and you'll get your longitude: 60°. Cross-reference that with your easily worked-out degrees of latitude, and you'll know exactly where you are. Simple? Yes and no.

A MATTER OF TECHNOLOGY

It's only simple if you have an accurate watch or clock. Back in the seventeenth and eighteenth centuries, a few people had accurate pendulum clocks in their houses but these certainly wouldn't work onboard ship! One roll of the deck and the pendulum would be useless. Even if they could somehow keep the clock upright and the pendulum swinging steadily, changes in temperature and **humidity** – quite apart from the dangers of salt water – would make the clock go haywire! So surely no one would have considered such a solution because there was no such thing as a marine chronometer ('ship-proof' clock).

TOUCH AND GO

Without being able to calculate their longitude at sea, experienced sailors reached their destinations through sighting familiar landmarks along the way, and sticking to pre-plotted courses as best they could. At worst, ships went dangerously off course, smashing on rocks they weren't expecting to be there. Down the years thousands of lives and ships were lost because of it. In 1675, King Charles II of England founded the Royal Observatory at Greenwich to try to solve the pressing problem of being able to find your longitude when out at sea. It was hoped that the movement of the moon in the sky, in relation to easily spotted stars, could create a kind of lunar clock that could be used by sailors. Results were slow in coming.

DISASTER!

Finally, the British Admiralty had enough. In 1707, over 2,000 men died when four ships went off course when returning to England and ran aground on the Scilly Isles. The British Board of Longitude was set up to tackle the problem and, in 1714, they offered a £20,000 prize. The prize would be awarded to whoever devised a method of pinpointing a ship's longitude anywhere on Earth to within an accuracy of half a degree (2 minutes of time). The British weren't only interested in saving lives, though. They also knew that the country which discovered the secret of calculating longitude at sea could 'rule the waves', and this would affect all trade, as well as military power.

A VARIETY OF SO-CALLED SOLUTIONS

£20,000 in 1714 would be the equivalent of well over a million pounds today so, not surprisingly, a great many people were interested in the Longitude Board's prize. There were some very wacky ideas indeed, though the Board itself suspected that there would be an astrological solution – that somehow it would be possible to work out longitude by plotting the course of the moon and stars. Others worked on pseudoscientific, almost magical solutions!

CRAZY AND CRUEL

One extraordinary suggestion was correctly based on the importance of knowing the time at $0°$ – but that was where the science ended and the craziness began. Here's what you had to do: first, injure a dog with a knife – sprinkled liberally with a special powder called the 'powder of sympathy' – then bandage the wound and take the dog onboard ship. Before you set sail, give an accomplice a set of the dog's bloody bandages. Once out at sea, part of your job is to make sure that the dog's wound never heals properly, and to listen out for the dog barking in pain on the hour, every hour, the time it was back in Greenwich. And how will the dog know when the hour is reached back

in Greenwich? Because of your accomplice, of course. They take the bloody bandage and dunk it in a solution of water and some more of that 'powder of sympathy', thus magically linking it to the original wound and causing the dog to cry out onboard ship. Of course, *every* ship would need a wounded dog and an accomplice back on shore, and, of course, it didn't work, but that's not to say that a number of countries didn't test out this fantastical approach!

A MATTER OF TIME

An Englishman named John Harrison (1693–1776), however, stuck with what he knew best: clocks. If one could design and build a clock that kept good time, even at sea, then the problem would be solved. It would, of course, have to be an extraordinary clock but, then again, Harrison was an extraordinary clockmaker. He even made some clocks out of wood. Yes; wood. The cogs and everything. The first clock that Harrison was ready to test at sea was quite remarkable. Completed in 1735, it looked and worked like no other clock before it and caused much interest. In 1736, Harrison took it on his own sea trials to Lisbon and back (out aboard the *Centurion* and back aboard the *Orford*). He was pleased with the results but, perfectionist that he was, decided to build an even better clock.

IMPROVEMENTS TO BE MADE

Whilst Harrison worked on, with funding from the Board, many Board members were hoping the solution lay elsewhere. What they were looking for was a clever naval solution involving charts of stars to guide them, preferably devised by a *gentleman*. They didn't want an amazingly simple mathematical solution based on an accurate 'marine chronometer' made by an uneducated clockmaker from the North! But Harrison didn't give up. In fact, he made it his life's work. He built version after version of his timepiece and was most pleased with the fourth: a much smaller, even more accurate clock, which looked like a giant fob watch. He finally completed it to his own satisfaction in 1759. In November 1761 it was carried aboard the *Deptford* by Harrison's son William, bound for Jamaica. The test of a trip to the West Indies was one of the original requirements of the competition. On arrival, William Harrison checked the watch. To be eligible for the prize, it mustn't be more than 2 minutes out (because this represented half a degree of longitude). As it turned out, it was less than 6 seconds slow!

A FINAL TEST

In a fair world, Harrison would probably have been awarded the prize there and then. As it was, the timepiece had to undergo *another* sea trial, aboard the *Tartar* bound for Barbados. Once again, Harrison's timepiece performed so well that it correctly predicted longitude to within half a degree. It worked! Harrison had discovered a way of accurately determining a ship's position, yet still the board were reluctant to pay him!

RECOGNITION AT LAST

After appeals to King George III himself, it was finally the British parliament, not the Board of Longitude, that paid John Harrison his prize money in 1773. And it was richly deserved. The famous explorer Captain Cook took a timepiece, based on Harrison's design, on his second voyage of exploration. He declared it a complete success. This was proof enough that Harrison had discovered a way for ships to pinpoint their positions so accurately that they could avoid all charted dangers. The whole point of offering the prize had been to give the British Navy the advantage if they found a solution – whilst other countries had to rely on latitude and guesswork alone. As it was, sailors everywhere benefited from the new system. In fact,

Harrison's method was used right up until recently by just about all navigators, until the advent of the Global Positioning System, where **satellites** can beam down a vessel's exact location onto a computer screen.

GERMS

6 JULY 1885, PARIS, FRANCE

Joseph Meister, a young boy, has been bitten fourteen times by a dog suspected to have rabies – a frightening disease which can cause foaming at the mouth, convulsions, paralysis and even death. Joseph's mother pleads with the scientist Louis Pasteur to give her son one of these vaccinations he's so famous for, but Pasteur has never tried out a rabies vaccination on a human patient before. Should he risk it? Has Joseph caught rabies from the bites? If not, Pasteur might actually give him rabies when trying to cure him. What should he do? He must decide. He must. Time is running out . . .

WHAT YOU CAN'T SEE . . .

When something is so well known and somehow seems so obvious, it's hard to imagine a time when people didn't know it too. A really good example of this is germs. It may seem hard to believe, but the existence of germs is a relatively recent discovery. Less than 200 years ago, nobody knew about them. Hospitals didn't change sheets between patients, and surgeons used the same implements on different patients, one after the other, without cleaning them. And this applied to clothes too. A surgeon would proudly wear a grimy, blood-stained apron to show just how many operations he'd performed! It didn't occur to people that rivers full of rubbish didn't make the best drinking water, or how diseases actually spread.

FIGHTING SMALLPOX WITH SMALLPOX

About 300 years ago, the most feared disease of all was smallpox. Beginning with a high fever, back and muscle pain, and often vomiting, smallpox then covered the victim's body in pus-filled blisters (or sores) and, usually, killed you. If, however, you were lucky enough to live, then

you couldn't catch it a second time . . . though you may
already have ended up scar-covered and blind. Doctors in
Turkey noticed this and had a very clever idea. If they
could deliberately give people a very mild form of
smallpox, which the people would then recover from, then
they might not get the disease again. But how to do it?
They collected the fluid from the blisters of smallpox
victims, scratched the arm of a healthy person and then
rubbed the fluid into it.

SPREADING THE WORD

The wife of the British Ambassador to Turkey was Lady
Mary Wortley Montagu. Afraid for her children's health
during the smallpox outbreak, and impressed with the logic
of what the doctors were trying, she had them treated this
way. Lady Montagu was famous for her letter-writing
(collections of them were later published in books), and she
took up the cause of encouraging British doctors back

home to try inoculating people against smallpox in this way. None dared try it. The British doctors thought the risk of actually giving a perfectly healthy person a killer dose of smallpox was too high, but Lady Montagu had planted a seed of an idea in their minds.

A DISCOVERY AND AN IDEA

The big breakthrough came when British doctor Edward Jenner (1749–1823) made an important discovery. As well as smallpox, there was a much milder disease called cowpox. Also known as *vaccinia*, this was a disease humans could catch from cows. They were both called 'poxes' because both diseases gave their victims fluid-filled blisters, but cowpox was very rarely fatal. In other words, victims of cowpox *lived*. What Jenner noticed was that people who'd had cowpox never seemed to get the deadly smallpox. The danger of the Turkish idea was that you could kill someone with that first dose of smallpox you were deliberately giving them. But what if you gave them a dose of the far-more-harmless *cow*pox instead? Might that have the same effect?

THE THEORY IS TESTED

In 1796, Edward Jenner found a milkmaid who'd caught cowpox from a cow. He took the fluid from one of the blisters on her hand and injected it into the arm of a perfectly healthy eight-year-old boy named James Phipps. James caught cowpox but wasn't seriously ill at all. Eight weeks later, Edward Jenner injected the boy again – this time with the deadly smallpox fluid. Fortunately for all concerned, James was fine. Although it was an extraordinarily risky experiment to try out on a child,

Jenner had discovered a way of beating smallpox.

THAT'S HOW, BUT WHY?

Our bodies have an immune system which fights to protect us against disease. When the cowpox was introduced into James Phipps's body, his immune system got to work at identifying what it was and finding a way of fighting it the best it could. (Sometimes our bodies fight a losing battle, when the disease wins and we die.) By the time that Jenner injected the smallpox, Phipps's immune system had 'learnt' how to tackle poxes, and so destroyed it. At first, people ridiculed Edward Jenner and his findings, particularly because he didn't know what caused smallpox, simply how to prevent it. The whole idea sounded crazy, but it soon became obvious that people inoculated with cowpox were surviving outbreaks of smallpox, whilst others died.

A STUNNING RESULT

The smallpox vaccination, as it became known, was one of the most remarkable achievements in medical history. From being one of the most feared and deadly diseases across the whole world, it now no longer exists. After mass smallpox vaccination programmes across whole continents, it was declared in 1979 that there hadn't been a single reported case of smallpox anywhere in the world. Anywhere! The only existing smallpox **virus** existed not in victims but in scientific research laboratories. It was agreed that these stocks should eventually be destroyed. Sadly, one of the last people to die from smallpox was an English scientist.

THE BRILLIANT MONSIEUR PASTEUR

The word 'virus' was one invented by Edward Jenner but 'vaccination' – named after cowpox, or vaccinia – wasn't. That was a term coined by Frenchman Louis Pasteur (1822–95), the man who really discovered germs and realized the role they played in diseases. Pasteur gained a reputation as a brilliant scientist and, in 1856, a Monsieur Bigo asked for his help. Monsieur Bigo's company made enormous amounts of alcohol, in huge vats of fermenting beet juice and a variety of vegetables. The only trouble was, it kept on going bad. Would Monsieur Pasteur look into the matter? Look into it he did, and the discovery he made and the conclusion he drew from it changed the world of medicine for ever.

THE MICRO WORLD OF MICROBES

Fermentation – the turning of fruit or vegetables into alcohol – was, in those days, thought to be a chemical reaction – where two or more substances interact together to produce a totally different product. When studied under a microscope, tiny, tiny blobs could be seen in the fermenting mixtures, but no real importance was attached to them. When Pasteur studied Monsieur Bigo's vats, however, he came to a startlingly different conclusion. He decided that these blobs were microbes: living things that could only be seen through a microscope. Furthermore, he decided that these particular microbes were yeasts (a kind of fungus, like toadstools and mushrooms). It was these yeast microbes, Pasteur argued, which turned the sugar into alcohol. Other scientists fell about laughing, until he performed a number of tests to prove it. Fermentation without the yeast microbes just didn't happen. Fermentation with different types of microbes simply spoiled the mixture. So Pasteur had not only solved Monsieur Bigo's particular problem but had also led to the science of microbiology!

GERM ATTACK!

But Louis Pasteur took his discoveries one stage further. One of the main groups of microbes that he studied were bacteria. He found them living all over the place: in water, in the soil, in plants and even in people. Some of these microbes – some of these bacteria – Pasteur now suggested, were harmful and he called these germs. Germs, he announced in a published work of 1858, caused illness and disease. One of the main arguments against this germ theory of disease was that the idea of these tiny living things somehow attacking and somehow killing much larger living things (in other words you and me) seemed ridiculous! How could a tiny plant or creature, or whatever it was, invade a human body from the outside and win?

The idea was preposterous. Preposterous or not, Pasteur had discovered the truth. It also went a long way to explaining why Jenner's vaccinations worked.

PASTEURIZATION

As Pasteur's reputation grew, he was asked by the Emperor of France, Napoleon III, to turn his attention to why so many French wines were turning sour. Pasteur quickly discovered that an invasion of the wrong types of microbe were the problem and, more importantly, that he could destroy them with heat. By heating wine (or beer) above 57°C (135°F) the germs would be killed but the taste and appearance unaffected. He then tried it on milk, which can contain many harmful bacteria, and it worked too. Today, in Britain, nearly all milk on sale is pasteurized (the name given to this process which, as you can see, was named after him). Again, here was another simple discovery that made all the difference.

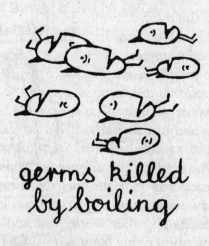

germs killed
by boiling

VACCINES

Over the years, Pasteur came to develop and understand many vaccines (which he named after the cowpox in recognition of Edward Jenner's earlier achievements) and even found a vaccine against rabies. It could only be given once patients had been bitten, but before they started showing any of the symptoms. When he tried it on badly bitten Joseph Meister in 1885, it saved the boy's life.

OTHER GREAT DISCOVERIES IN MEDICINE

In the fight against germs another great advance came in 1847. Many mothers and new-born babies suffered from 'childbed' or puerperal fever, which often spread from house to house. A Hungarian doctor called Ignaz Semmelweiss came up with the solution. He said that it might be a good idea if doctors present at childbirth *washed their hands* before and after delivering the baby! The reduction in the spread of the fever was dramatic. British surgeon Joseph Lister came up with an even more effective method of germ prevention. He had discovered that carbolic acid (usually a white crystal dissolved in water) acted as a germ-killer, and began using it in surgery. Lister had discovered antiseptic, another weapon in the

doctors please wash hands

fight against germs. The discovery of germs and how to defeat them has changed our world completely, saving millions upon millions of lives and transforming the levels of hygiene and quality of life across the globe. The discovery of anaesthetics and antibiotics were to have a startling effect too, as you can see in the next chapter.

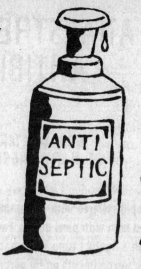

ANAESTHETICS AND ANTIBIOTICS

1928, BACTERIOLOGY LAB, ST MARY'S HOSPITAL, LONDON

Alexander Fleming's laboratory is as cluttered as always. Every worktop is covered with something, and the sink in the laboratory is piled high with petri dishes. Each petri dish – small, round and with a tightly fitting lid – contains bacteria, used as part of Fleming's experiments on flu germs. Back from his summer holiday, Fleming is opening each petri dish in turn, looking at the bacteria and then soaking it in cleaning solution, until . . . he notices one of the petri dishes has something furry growing in it – some kind of mould. These things happen. The lid can't have been on properly. Tests sometimes get contaminated and spoiled. Then Fleming looks closer, with a mixture of scientific interest and mounting excitement. There's no bacteria around the edge of the mould, it's all to the side. Could this mysterious mould have somehow killed these germs? And what exactly is it?

mysterious mould →

TAKE AWAY THE PAIN

As well as those remarkable discoveries in the previous chapter, there have been many other advances in medicine, but, probably, none more so than antibiotics: the drugs that can tackle all sorts of different germs. But, before their discovery, came another milestone in medical treatment: anaesthetics. Anaesthetics help to deaden pain – either by putting the patient to sleep (a general anaesthetic) or by numbing the area to be operated on (a local anaesthetic). Before their discovery and use, patients would usually be wide awake when their legs were amputated or their bodies cut open. Patients were often soldiers or sailors injured in fighting, and they might be lucky enough to have had a smoke of hemp (which is a plant also used for making ropes) or a swig of rum to relax them – but it would still have been agony, and they would have to have been held down on the table. Early general anaesthetics included laughing gas and a liquid called ether. The trouble with ether was that it was difficult to know how much to give to the patient for it to be effective. Patients often woke up halfway through being operated on, or were very sick afterwards. In 1831, an American chemist called Samuel Guthrie created a drug called chloroform but it wasn't used in an operation for sixteen years.

A ROYAL THUMBS-UP

Scottish surgeon James Simpson was eager to find a way to make operations less painful and frightening for his patients, but wasn't happy with ether. He knew about the waking-up-early and being-violently-sick **side effects** so, in 1847, he thought he should try this chloroform he'd heard about. But who should he try it out on? In the end, he decided to take the chloroform himself, along with two other doctors (Dr Duncan and Dr Keith). This they did – and all immediately collapsed to the floor, asleep. Though sleeping, Dr Keith kept kicking the bottom of a table with his feet, and waving his arms about. The other two doctors lay as still as two sacks of potatoes. When they finally woke up, Simpson declared his rather unusual experiment a complete success! It wasn't until Queen Victoria was given chloroform in 1853 when giving birth to her eighth child – she had nine altogether, and the eighth one was Leopold – that it suddenly caught on and became all the rage.

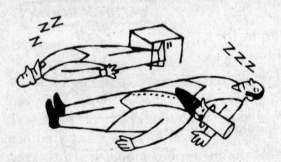

X-RAYS

Another remarkable discovery for the medical profession was the X-ray in 1895. Discovered accidentally by the German physicist Wilhelm Roentgen, X-rays can take photographs of the inside of a person's body: bones and inner organs. This way, many problems can be revealed without the doctor having to cut the patient open. One of the problems with actually operating on a patient, you see, is the added risk of infection. An operation might cure them of one thing, and promptly kill them with germs! This is why one of the greatest life-savers of all was the discovery of antibiotics – drugs which can kill all sorts of different types of germs, rather than one particular type.

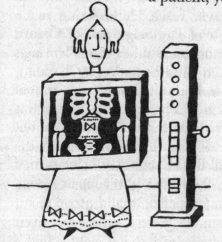

ALEXANDER FLEMING

In 1922, Alexander Fleming discovered a natural antiseptic in tears, but he is best remembered for his discovery of the first known antibiotic: penicillin. The importance of this discovery becomes clear when you realize that penicillin could even have prevented the bubonic plague epidemics in the Middle Ages, which killed millions of people! When Fleming discovered penicillin – for that was the mysterious mould he discovered on the petri dish at the start of this chapter – it didn't cause much excitement or interest when he published his findings. Fleming himself worked on the mould, but growing it in reasonable amounts proved very difficult. So here was a potentially life-saving wonder drug that was largely being ignored.

FLOREY AND CHAIN

All that was about to change, thanks to pathologist Howard Walter Florey. Florey was born in Australia but came to England to study and, later, teach. After being made director of the Dunn School of Pathology, part of Oxford University, in 1935, he began studies on Fleming's penicillin mould. By 1939, he and Ernst Boris Chain – a Jewish German who'd left Berlin following the rise of Nazism – had not only found which part of the mould was the active, germ-killing ingredient, but had also worked out ways of producing more of the drug. Then came the Second World War. With all British resources being turned to the war effort, and with the British government having no idea just how important penicillin would prove to be, Florey went to the USA.

TAKING PENICILLIN

One of the problems with penicillin in this original form was that you couldn't simply swallow it because all its 'healing' powers were destroyed by digestive juices before it could have any effect. You couldn't be given penicillin in an injection because, at this stage, it contained too many other impurities that might do you more harm than good. Florey and Chain managed to produce pure penicillin, but in very small amounts. In early tests on a patient, penicillin was in such short supply that it had to be chemically extracted from the patient's urine and used again! In the USA, eventually enough penicillin was produced to help the fight against germs infecting wounded soldiers, and its true worth was proved. Even then, it was cheaper and easier to make the drug from enormous vats of fermenting mould than to produce it chemically in a laboratory. Today, however, it can be mass-produced chemically, both cheaply and effectively.

HIGHEST HONOURS

The war ended in 1945, the same year that Alexander Fleming, Howard Walter Florey and Ernst Chain were jointly awarded the Nobel Prize for Medicine – Fleming, for realizing the importance, if not the possibilities, of his accidental discovery, and Florey and Chain for turning these possibilities into a life-saving reality. A variety of antibiotics have been widely available since the 1950s and what were once considered life-threatening diseases are now treatable. Pneumonia and TB (tuberculosis), which used to be the deadliest of diseases, can now be cured. And more and more complicated operations can be carried out thanks to antibiotics too, now that there's less chance of those dreaded infections. In the past, many simple operations were surgically successful – what needed putting right was put right – but then the patient died from infection. Not so today. Antibiotics have changed the world of medicine almost beyond recognition.

GENETICS

8 MARCH 1965, BRÜNN SOCIETY FOR THE STUDY OF NATURAL SCIENCE

Gregor Mendel stands before the assembled audience. The paper he has just read contains information that could completely alter the understanding of biology as we know it. His research, discoveries and conclusions could rock the very foundations of existing beliefs on human life itself – if only someone was interested. The guests had come here expecting to hear a talk on plants, instead, he's given them a talk on genetics and they just don't understand what he's told them. Have all his years of painstaking hard work really gone to waste?

Gregor Johann Mendel (1822–84) was a man whose brilliance was never recognized in his own lifetime but whose discoveries were later – *much* later – taken up by others and, without a doubt, changed the world. Mendel was an Austrian born to a poor peasant family in what is now the Czech Republic. He later became a monk in an Augustinian monastery at Brünn (also now in the Czech Republic) which, even then, had a reputation for being a place of scientific learning. After studying at the University of Vienna, he failed to get a teaching degree and returned to the monastery as an abbot. There, he began his years of careful experimentation.

PEAS, GLORIOUS PEAS

Between 1856 and 1863, Mendel grew and cross-bred over 28,000 pea plants of different varieties. He studied

everything from the heights of the various plants to the shape of the pods and the peas within them and the colours of their flowers. Then he bred tall plants with short plants, smooth pea plants with knobbly pea plants, white-flowered plants with purple-flowered plants, straight podded plants with bent podded plants. You name it, he tried it. He then studied the **offspring** pea plants this cross-breeding created, and made some very important discoveries.

TALL PLANT, SHORT PLANT

Using the heights of the plants as an example – either tall or short – here's what he discovered. If tall plants were only bred with other tall plants, you only ever got tall plants. And breeding short plants with short plants (pure-breeding) always resulted in short plants. If you cross-bred pure-bred tall plants with pure-bred short plants, however, you always ended up with tall offspring too – *never* short ones. Next, Mendel crossbred these new offspring (with one tall and one short parent) and made an interesting discovery. Although the new parents were all tall, for every three tall offspring they had, they had one short one. (This is called a ratio of 3 to 1, or 3:1). Mendel worked out why.

A PAIR OF GENES

He suggested that each parent plant had a pair of (what we now call) genes. For example, a pure-bred tall plant had two 'tall' height genes (which we'll show as TT) and a pure-bred small plant had two 'small' height genes (which we'll show as SS). But, he went on, each parent must only give *one* gene from the pair to their offspring (one T or one S). This meant that the offspring of TT (tall) and SS (short) parents would always end up with one of four combinations of the TS genes. Because all the offspring turned out tall, T must be a stronger, more dominant gene than small's S. Mendel called this 'dominance'. When these TS offspring had offspring of their own, though, why was every fourth plant small, Mendel wondered? Because the height genes of two TS parent plants combining leave you with TT TS ST SS – and where there's no dominant tall T height gene and just two small SS height genes, the plant has no option than to be small!

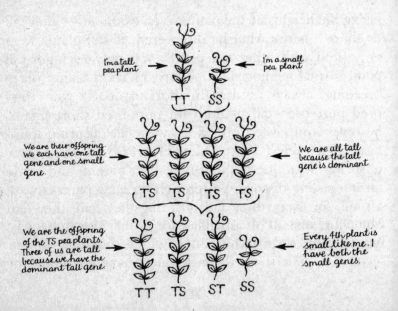

I'm a tall pea plant

I'm a small pea plant

TT SS

We are their offspring. We each have one tall gene and one small gene.

We are all tall because the tall gene is dominant.

TS TS TS TS

We are the offspring of the TS pea plants. Three of us are tall because we have the dominant tall gene.

Every 4th plant is small like me. I have both the small genes.

TT TS ST SS

REGRESSIVENESS

What was so important about this was that although the offspring of the crossbred pure-bred tall and pure-bred small plants all appeared to be tall, they all had the short, less dominant height gene in them which did nothing *until they too had offspring*. This gene would then be able to reappear in every fourth offspring (which Mendel called 'regressing', in other words 'going back to being' as short as one of its grandparents). So Mendel had not only discovered that the parents had pairs of genes for different functions, and only gave one from each pair, but also discovered dominant and regressive genes – and this doesn't just apply to plants and animals but to you and me too, with everything from eyes to hair colour!

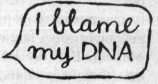

TOO CLEVER BY HALF

Mendel's Laws are still the basis for genetic research today but, in 1866, they were so ahead of his time that no one seemed to understand them, let alone take any notice of his published results or talks. Part of the problem was that he explained his ideas with numbers and statistics, rather than as simply as possible. In 1900, a number of people picked up on his discoveries and began to realize their importance, but it wasn't until even later that their full significance was discovered.

DNA

We now know that the nucleus of every human cell contains a DNA **molecule**. 'DNA' is short for 'deoxyribonucleic acid'. *Very* short for 'deoxyribonucleic acid', which is why everyone, including scientists, usually refers to it as 'DNA'. DNA contains the genes, or instructions, that pass on characteristics from one generation of a family to the next, in the same way that Mendel's peas did. As long ago as 1869, scientists realized that there was DNA in our cells, but they weren't very sure what it did, or what the molecule actually looked like.

THE BUILDING BLOCKS OF LIFE

By the 1950s, scientists had reached the startling conclusion that DNA was a very complicated molecule made up of much simpler ones, which can be imagined as the 'building blocks of life'. Put the blocks together in a different order and you get a different form of life, because all living things – plants or animals – contain DNA. The only problem was that scientists didn't actually yet know the structure of DNA and how it reproduced itself, to pass on to the next generation.

DISCOVERING THE DOUBLE HELIX

The two people responsible for calculating that the DNA molecule is a double helix in shape – once described to me as being a bit like a rope ladder being twisted into a spiral – were the British scientist Francis Crick and the American scientist James Watson, in 1953. Although they were the ones who made this public breakthrough, they did it based on scientific data from two other British scientists: the physicist Maurice Wilkins and crystallographer Rosalind Franklin. Rosalind Franklin's data was shown to Crick and Watson without her knowledge, including a photograph she had managed to take of a DNA molecule, the only one in existence. Sadly, she did not receive the Nobel Prize with Crick, Watson and Wilkins. She had died of cancer by the time they were given this great honour.

GENETIC ENGINEERING

Once DNA had been understood in this way, many scientists wanted to see what would happen if they moved around these 'building blocks of life'. This process is called genetic engineering: altering nature – whether plants or animals – to, supposedly, help humankind. This was first achieved, at a very basic level, in 1973 in the USA.

DOLLY THE CLONE

Today, genetic engineering is very rarely out of the news. Cloning has also become a reality. Once the stuff of science fiction, it is now possible to create one living, breathing animal from the cell of another, without need for 'parents'. The first example of this was Dolly the sheep, first revealed to the world in 1997. Dolly, named after the country singer

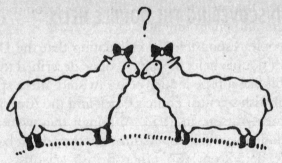

Dolly Parton, was cloned from the single cell of an adult sheep by Dr Ian Wilmut in Scotland. Many fear that human cloning will one day take place. Some people believe that this would be morally and ethically wrong.

FRANKENSTEIN FOODS

Another area of genetics causing a great deal of controversy is genetically modified crops and food. Some scientists believe that, by subtly changing the genetic make-up of some foods, they can be made bigger, or more **nutritious** or more resistant to disease, for example. Such altered crops are said to be genetically modified or GM crops. Many people who are opposed to scientists supposedly 'tampering with nature' call them 'Frankenstein food' after the character of Dr Frankenstein, who created a monster. These people

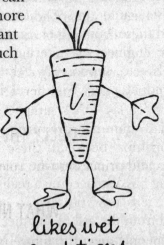

likes wet conditions

are concerned that genetically modified crops could upset the ecosystem and environment.

flies off
the tree

DNA FINGERPRINTING

In the 1980s, another important and completely different use for DNA was discovered: people can be 'genetically fingerprinted'. Everyone's fingerprints are unique and, if left at a crime scene, can be matched against a suspect's prints taken at the police station. Genetic 'fingerprints' aren't really fingerprints at all, but can help match up a suspect with a crime. For example, the saliva on an apple eaten at a crime scene can be checked for DNA and compared against another DNA sample taken from a suspect. Today, DNA samples taken from 3,000 year-old Egyptian mummies are being used to work out the family relationships between these dead pharaohs, queens, princes and princesses who ruled that ancient civilization!

WHAT NEXT?

Some people view the future of genetic engineering with great excitement, believing that it might be possible to clone human organs so that diseased or destroyed organs – such as hearts and livers, for example – can be replaced without the need for donors. Others fear that it may lead to 'eugenics' – the careful manipulation of genes to create 'perfect' people, the sex that you want, the size that you want with the hair and colour of eyes that you want – rather than letting nature take its course. The discovery of DNA and genetics has certainly opened up whole new horizons – and a can of worms!

PLASTICS

1907, HUDSON RIVER VALLEY, NEW YORK STATE, USA

The son of a Belgian shoemaker, American chemist Leo Hendrik Baekeland has already made his fortune selling his photographic paper, Velox, to George Eastman of Kodak for $750,000 in 1899. Now he is hard at work on a new challenge in his laboratory, the converted stable block of his home, Snug Rock. Baekeland has spent five years trying to produce a plastic, using substances extracted from coal tar and wood alcohol, and for year after year all he's come up with is a useless mass of goo. Until now! At last, at long last, he's produced a resin that doesn't burn, melt or dissolve once hardened into shape. He's developed the world's first practical synthetic plastic!

A RECENT DISCOVERY

Today, so many things are made of colourful, lightweight, tough, easily moulded plastics that it's quite hard to imagine – or, if you're older, to *remember* – life without them. It's not that long ago that people listened to music on records, not CDs, and what were those earliest records (called 78s) made from? Plastic? Wrong. They were made from beetle secretions. Yup, you read that right. Records used to be made of a kind of resin squeezed out of lac beetles and called shellac. (It's said to have taken 15,000 beetles six months to produce just 453 grams' (1 lb') worth, so you can imagine how expensive it was!) Fortunately for us, and for the beetles, the discovery of plastics has changed all that. Today, everything from light switches to artificial hips are made of plastic!

EASY TO USE

Plastics are light, hard-wearing and easy to clean, but also tough, waterproof and cheap to make. They don't rust or rot either – which can be a good thing and a bad thing – and they can easily be made into just about any shape. Plastic is a name given to materials which have giant, organic molecules – I'll explain more about that later, have no fear – that can be formed into just about any shape we want, using a variety of different methods.

EYES ON THE PRIZE

In 1860, a firm which made ivory billiard and pool balls in the USA offered a $10,000 prize for anyone who could come up with a substitute for the ivory. Inventor John Wesley Hyatt discovered a way of producing a transparent, colourless plastic which could be easily dyed and moulded. This was the very first plastic and Hyatt called it celluloid. He didn't win the prize, but he did have great success with celluloid. It did have two drawbacks though. First, a British inventor claimed that he'd already come up with the same plastic, but had called it xylonite. Secondly, celluloid was highly flammable: it caught fire very easily and, when it burnt, it *really* burnt! One of its main uses was for camera film. Today, a more fire-resistant version of celluloid is

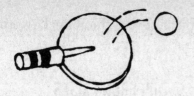

probably most commonly used for ping-pong balls.

THE BAKELITE BREAKTHROUGH

Then Baekeland discovered his way of producing the first **thermosetting** plastic in about 1907 and soon everything from wirelesses – what we'd now call radios and which, up until then had been in wooden cases – to cameras, pens and telephones were made from it. Plastic is a good **insulator**, so is ideal for casing electrical products. Rather than bright colours, Bakelite was usually black, brown or tortoiseshell and was very brittle. It cracked easily if knocked too hard. Baekeland became fabulously rich and sold his company and retired to Florida in 1939. Finding the climate hot, he used to enjoy standing fully clothed in his swimming pool!

BUILDING THOSE CHAINS

The 1920s and 1930s saw major discoveries and breakthroughs in the understanding of plastics – that small molecules (often referred to as monomers) can be linked together to create long-chain molecules and that these long-chain molecules can be linked to other long-chain molecules to create really, *really* big molecules of stretchy, mouldable plastics. Molecules made of linked-up

81

monomers are called polymers, from the Greek word 'poly', meaning 'many bits'.

DIFFERENT PLASTICS, DIFFERENT USES

One of the great things about plastics is that scientists soon discovered that, by mixing and matching different monomers to make different polymers, they could create different types of plastics for different uses. For example, some plastics soften and melt when they're heated because their polymers – long chain molecules – are side-by-side rather than all linked together. These are called thermoplastics. Other types of plastics, called thermosetting plastics, don't melt because their polymers are tightly linked.

POLYTHENE, PVC and POLYPROPYLENE

A good example of two very common and different types of plastic are polythene and PVC. Polythene can be made as thin as paper and is ideal for using as a transparent film to wrap food in. PVC, on the other hand, is much tougher and can be used to make everything from trousers to luggage. Polythene was developed by the German scientist Karl Zieglar in 1953. He shared the Nobel Prize for Chemistry with Giulo Natta (the developer of polypropylene) in 1963 for their work on polymers and plastics. Polypropylene is a thermoplastic which is ideal for making anything from bottles to brush bristles to carpets.

THE RAW MATERIALS

The earliest plastics were made from substances discovered in milk, coal, cotton and even wood. Today, the most important basic ingredients for plastics come from oil. The oil which comes up out of the ground when drilled – the thick, black gooey liquid – is called crude oil. This is then heated up in a fractionating (separating) tower in an oil refinery. The heat causes the crude oil to separate into different types of liquid which are, in turn, used to create different products. These are mainly fuels: petrol, diesel oil and paraffin, but also a liquid called naphtha. It is this naphtha which is used in the plastics process. It is reheated to create a substance called ethylene, from which millions of polyethylene chips (plastic pellets) are produced.

SHAPING PLASTICS

Plastics can be shaped into objects in a variety of different ways. The most obvious is moulding, where hot, liquid plastic is poured into a mould and air is blown into the mould (pressing the plastic to the sides). Then, when the plastic has cooled down and become hard, the mould is opened and the plastic removed. It's taken on the shape of the mould, but is hollow inside – ideal for everything from bottles to footballs. Another method, extrusion, is when hot, melted plastic is forced through a hole of the desired shape and size, which when cool and hard makes long hollow tubes – for pipes, guttering etc. By blowing gas bubbles into melted plastic, hard or soft foam plastics can be made. One of the most common plastic foams is polystyrene, often used to make fast-food containers.

PLASTIC CLOTHES

If all you think of are plastic macs and PVC jackets and trousers when you think of plastic clothes, think again. Plastics can actually be made into long, thin threads and woven into garments. To make the plastic threads, melted plastic is forced through tiny holes in a machine – a bit like the rose on the end of a watering can – called a spinneret. Whilst still warm, these threads can be stretched even further and thinner. The first and most famous of these plastic threads is nylon, which came about as the result of research and experiments by one Wallace Carothers.

WALLACE CAROTHERS

American scientist Wallace Carothers (1896–1937) was such a brilliant chemistry student that his college asked him to become a teacher! He later went on to become a teacher at Harvard, the most prestigious university in the USA, but was persuaded to leave and join the DuPont company in 1928 as head of research in organic chemistry. It was at DuPont that Carothers and his team of eight worked on long-chain polymers in a special lab set up to study 'pure science'. They nicknamed the building Purity Hall.

A BIT OF LUCK

It was in Purity Hall that, one day in 1930, a member of Carothers's team – Julian Hill – looked into a vat containing one of Carothers's polymer resins and dipped a glass rod in it, to give it a prod. Pulling the rod out, he found the resin stuck to the end of it and, as he walked backwards across the room, he was amazed to find that it stretched out into a long plastic thread! When news got out that Carothers's team were on their way to developing a human-made plastic that could be woven into clothes, there was much excitement. The problem was, if washed or ironed, the new fibre melted into a horrible gooey mess. More work certainly needed to be done!

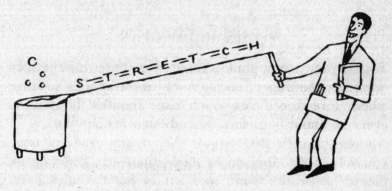

NYLON

The breakthrough came in 1934 when Carothers developed a new approach for synthesizing these giant polymers, resulting in a strong plastic fibre which didn't melt below 195° C. It originally appeared on the market as toothbrush bristles under the name of Exton! In 1938, DuPont finally announced that their laboratories had produced 'the first man-made organic

textile fabric prepared entirely from new materials from the mineral kingdom'. They called it 'nylon' and nylon stockings first went on sale in 1940. They were a huge success. Sadly, Carothers didn't live to see this. Less than three weeks after DuPont filed for a **patent** on nylon, he killed himself by drinking the poison cyanide. Despite his incredible discoveries and achievements, Carothers often felt depressed and a failure. He'd had a breakdown and even spent time in a sanatorium. In his short life, however, he certainly left a lasting legacy.

PLUSES AND MINUSES

You only have to sit inside a modern car to see how plastics dominate the lives of so many of us today. The steering wheel, gear knob, dashboard, door handles, head rests, even the paint – in fact, just about *everything* you see – contains plastics. But, despite their many excellent uses, you only have to look on a rubbish tip to see the problems plastics cause the world too. Unlike natural substances, such as paper or wood, they decompose very slowly (if at all). Very few plastics are biodegradable (in other words, they're not broken down by bacteria when buried). So plastics have done much to pollute our world too. The solution probably lies in recycling: old, unwanted plastic items being collected, cleaned and sorted and melted down to make new ones or, better still, reusing items such as plastic bags rather than throwing them away first time. Plastics are like so many of the other discoveries in this book. It's what people do with them that makes such a difference – good or bad – to our planet.

INVENTIONS
that Changed the World

For Frederick Ardagh,
the grandfather I never knew

INVENTIONS!

Imagine a world where no one has discovered electricity ... or a world where electricity has been discovered, but the inventors didn't know what to do with it! There would be no telephones, radios, televisions, computer games, internet ... the list goes on and on. Think how different the whole history of the world would be without these, and other, great inventions. Without the invention of aeroplanes and, later, the jet engine, for example, a journey from Britain to Australia could take a very – and I mean *very* – long time. Now, nowhere in the world is more than 24 hours away in the fastest planes. In this *WOW!* book, we take a look at some of the most fantastic inventions that changed the world, along with what led up to their invention and what came afterwards. As for what the future has in store, who knows? As these past inventions show, what seems impossible today could easily become a reality tomorrow. Just you wait and see or, better still, get inventing!

PHILIP ARDAGH
2000

THE TELEPHONE

10 MARCH 1875, BOSTON, MASSACHUSETTS, USA

Scottish-born inventor Alexander Graham Bell is tired but excited. After years of work, he's ready to put his telephonic apparatus to the test. With his assistant, Thomas Watson, eagerly waiting by a second phone in the other room, Bell prepares himself for what he hopes will be a historic moment ... but, then, disaster strikes. Acid from the battery powering his equipment spills onto his trousers and Bell leaps to his feet. "Mr Watson! Come here! I want you!" he cries, unaware that he is speaking into the mouthpiece. He has just made the world's very first telephone call.

A MARATHON RUN

How we can communicate with each other beyond shouting distance is something that people have been puzzling over for a very long time indeed. One obvious solution was using runners. A runner could memorize an important message from one person and run off and repeat it to another. Once reading and writing was more widely developed, a runner could actually carry a written message. An ancient Greek runner, sometimes referred to as Pheidippides, ran non-stop all the way from the Plain of Marathon to the city of Athens in 490BC – over 23 miles (37 kilometres) – with the message that the Athenians had defeated their Persian enemies in battle. He was so exhausted, he promptly dropped down dead, which was a shame. This exhausting run from Marathon is still remembered today, in marathon races (of over 26 miles – 42 kilometres).

DON'T SHOOT THE MESSENGER!

Other early runners, or messengers, often ended up dead for another reason: a tradition developed in some societies that deliverers of bad news should be killed. This was more than a teeny-weenie bit unfair – because they were just doing their jobs! – which is how we come to have the phrase 'Don't shoot the messenger'. (In other words, it's the *news* that's bad, not the poor person who brings it.)

A RIGHT ROYAL MALE

You can see how, over thousands of years, the system of messengers running here, there and everywhere with written messages developed into the postal service. In England, King Henry VIII (yes, he with the big belly and six wives) appointed a Master of the Post in 1516. These posts were 'staging posts', in other words they were places where a postmaster (usually an innkeeper) was responsible

for passing a piece of mail on to the next post, and so on, down the line. And, in case you haven't guessed it, this is where we get the terms 'post office' and 'postage' from. (You can impress your friends by casually mentioning this in conversation.) Later, these staging posts became stop-off points for mail coaches, where the postman could rest or change his horses. Later still, came postal workers with bicycles, vans, trains, ships and even aeroplanes.

GOT IT LICKED

The idea, in Britain, that a letter should cost the same to deliver wherever it was sent on the mainland came into being in 1840. Before that, the further a message went, the more you paid – which was bad luck if you lived in Cornwall and your granny lived in Scotland. At the same time, the world's first stick-on stamps were issued: the

Penny Blacks. As their name suggests, they were black (with Queen Victoria's head on them in white) and cost an old penny each.

SMOKE AND FLAMES

But written messages delivered by others weren't the only way people could communicate without being face to face. Other obvious approaches included fires and smoke signals. A series of fires (called beacons) were lit around the coastline of England to warn of the coming of the Spanish Armada invasion force in 1588. When the ships were spotted and the alarm raised, a beacon was lit and, when the fire from that beacon was spotted by those at the next beacon, they lit theirs and so on. On the other hand, smoke signals – popularly used by some Native Americans – could be used to send more complicated messages. Different puffs of smoke meant different things so the receiver had to be able to 'read' them. Whereas a burning beacon signal meant just one pre-arranged thing – 'the enemy is coming!' – different smoke signals sent different messages.

FLAGGING IT UP

A popular system of ship-to-ship and ship-to-shore communications used to be flags. Traditionally, ships flew their countries' flags so other ships would know whether they were friend or foe – and we all know what a skull-and-crossbones means – but other, smaller, shipboard flags were combined to make messages too. In battle, the flagship could hoist flags to send orders, which could be read through telescopes by those aboard other ships of the fleet. In one famous incident, at the battle of Copenhagen, Admiral Horatio Nelson was informed that the signal on the flagship was ordering withdrawal. Not wanting to quit fighting, he's said to have put his telescope up to his blind eye, covered in a patch and said, 'I really do not see the signal' – which was very naughty, but Nelson was a bit of an all-round hero and good guy, so history has decided that that's all right then! Flags are still used today, of course, but in friendlier 'battles', such as greeting the winner of a Grand Prix race with the chequered flag, or by linespeople at football and rugby matches, trying to catch the ref's eye.

IN A FLAP

Another, more complicated, system of signal-sending using flags – called semaphore – was developed. Here, whole messages could be spelt out letter by letter, with each letter formed by two flags being held out in particular positions. Short cuts were developed so, for example, a semaphore message from someone in big trouble and needing help could be shortened to SOS ('Save Our Souls').

THE STARTING WIRE

All of the approaches mentioned so far were certainly impressive, but the real problem was the *time* it took to send a message over any great distance. All this was about to change with the invention of the telegraph – a way of sending coded electrical signals down a wire. (They weren't coded so that people couldn't understand them but because it was assumed that a human voice couldn't be crammed down a telegraph wire, so the message had to be spelled out somehow.) A number of different people were working **independently** on the telegraph, with the first public telegraph lines being laid in England between Paddington and Slough in 1843 and in the USA between Washington DC and Baltimore, Maryland in 1844. But it was the American inventor Samuel Morse, the 'father' of the telegraph, who turned it into such a brilliantly useful device.

ON THE DOT

It was Morse who invented Morse Code. (If his name had been Mr Cod it might have been called Cod Code.) In the same way that **software** is such an important part of computers, the way messages could be sent down the telegraph were what made the telegraph so successful. Instead of semaphore, Morse relied on electric dots and dashes to make up his alphabet. In Morse code, SOS started out as three quick taps (or 'dots') for the 'S', followed by three slower 'dashes' for the 'O', followed by three quick 'dots' for the 'S' again. The dots and dashes were tapped out by the telegraph sender, sent electrically down the telegraph wire and picked up by the receiver in his headphones. (There were even competitions to see who could send and receive telegraphed Morse messages the quickest.) The world's first telegraphed Morse Code message was sent on 24 May 1844 by Morse himself. It read: 'What hath God wrought!' which was a bit serious, but this was a serious occasion. Just think about it. A message from Missouri to California that might take ten days to be delivered by the **Pony Express**, could now be delivered – zzzzzzzzip! – at the speed of light.

RING IN THE CHANGES

It was whilst experimenting with a telegraph machine that Alexander Graham Bell (1847–1922) developed the idea for a telephone – a machine that would convert speech into electrical energy, which could be sent great distances. A Scotsman, Bell moved to Canada and then the US, in 1871. (He later became a US citizen.) In 1875, he founded a school in Boston, Massachusetts, for 'deaf-mutes' and was a speech teacher, fascinated by the human voice. (You can find out more about how a telephone actually works on page 101.) The phone wasn't his only invention either. He came up with the first electric hearing aid in 1846.

MAKING A CASE

Amazingly, just a few hours after Bell had filed a **patent** for the telephone, another inventor, by the name of Elisha Gray, filed a claim that *he* had already invented a telephone and that Bell shouldn't be given a patent. Various other inventors claimed to have invented the telephone before Bell too, but none of them could ever actually prove it in court! Poor old Bell had to defend his rights to the phone about 600 times before the Supreme Court of the United States finally officially pronounced, once and for all, that Bell did, indeed, invent it.

THE TELEPHONE REVOLUTION

It's not difficult to see how the telephone changed the world. Now, two people on opposite sides of the world can talk to each other, without bleeps, dots, dashes, flashes or flags, and it's so quick and easy. Getting in touch with someone the other side of the world is often as simple as picking up a phone and punching in a few numbers. Imagine how long it would take using old methods, with runners, horses, boats – it could be a matter of months, not minutes. And then you'd still have to wait at least as long for the reply! Now documents can be 'faxed' down phone lines – where a duplicate (or a **facsimile**) of a document can be reproduced on a fax machine anywhere in the world. By fitting a modem to a computer, phone lines can take on a whole new function. A modem converts the digital bits of a computer's output into an audio tone. This is then encoded as an electrical signal which is sent through telephone lines to be decoded by a modem fitted to a computer at the receiving end. Hey presto! You've got e-mail and everything the internet has to offer. The telephone is one mind-boggling, world-changing invention.

99

RECORDED SOUND

DECEMBER 1877, MENLO PARK, NEW YORK, USA

Thomas Edison, already famous for many other inventions, sits himself down by a strange-looking contraption he has called the phonograph. Designed by him but built by his colleague John Kruesi, Edison is about to put the machine through an early test. Placing his lips to the mouthpiece he recites the nursery rhyme 'Mary Had a Little Lamb'. Moments later, he plays the words back on the machine. He has managed to capture the human voice!

LOST AND GONE FOR EVER

Before writing, songs and stories were passed by word of mouth. You heard something. You tried to remember it. You repeated it and passed it on. Of course, you could never repeat it *exactly*. Then came writing. Now a song or a story could be written down. It could be read note for note and word for word. But, again, you could never repeat someone else's version of a song or the way they spoke a story *exactly*. Once that moment of singing or speaking was gone, it was gone for ever. Even musical instruments are

played differently by different musicians and no two performances by the same musician are ever identical.

THE MAGIC KEYBOARD

The Pianola, a special mechanical piano, was a brilliant invention of the 1890s, because it actually played piano tunes *on a piano*. You could sit at home and listen to music coming out of your Pianola – with the keys moving before your eyes, as though being played by an invisible pianist! In fact, inside the Pianola, the keys were pressed down by air pressure from bellows. The airflow was controlled by perforations – small holes – in a large paper roll. As the roll moved, the air blew through the holes onto the right keys. Load the Pianola with a different paper roll, the air from the bellows would blow through different holes and different notes would play out a different tune. Magic!

GOOD VIBRATIONS

Sound is **vibration**. Speak into a telephone mouthpiece, to a friend, for example, and the **diaphragm** (a small, circular, very thin disc, pronounced 'dia-fram') vibrates, altering the magnetic field around a magnet, turning these vibrations into an electrical signal. This electrical signal passes down the phone wire, alters a magnetic field around a magnet in the receiver of your friend's phone which, in turn, recreates the original vibrations in a diaphragm in their earpiece. And your friend hears your voice – all in a fraction of a second. Which is fiendishly clever and fiendishly simple, all at once!

101

EDISON ON THE CASE

Alexander Graham Bell had made the first phone call in 1875, but Thomas Edison (1847–1931) was working on an 'improved' version of the telephone in 1877. Watching a diaphragm vibrate, he wondered if it would be somehow possible to record those vibrations. He attached a **stylus** to the diaphragm so, when he spoke, the diaphragm would vibrate and make the stylus move up and down, creating tiny dents on a piece of paper. He tested this by saying the word 'Halloo!' Now he had the dents on the paper, he passed the paper back under the stylus, causing it to bob up and down and, in turn, make the diaphragm vibrate. In other words, he was trying to 'play' the sound he had recorded by simply reversing the process he'd used to record the dents on the paper. Although Edison was the first to admit that you needed 'strong imagination' to hear the original 'Halloo!', he could certainly hear something, and he knew that he was on to something *big*.

THE FIRST RECORDER

Rumours reached Edison that there were other inventors trying to come up with ways to record sound, so there was no time to lose. When he designed the first phonograph, he decided that the stylus must make dents on a revolving cylinder covered in metal foil rather than paper. This should pick up the dents from the vibrations far more clearly. It worked! It worked! Soon, these metal foil cylinders were replaced by wax ones and phonographs sold the world over. (In Britain, they were called gramophones, and you still hear some older people talk about 'gramophone records' today.)

IT'S A RECORD!

The first machines to record and play flat discs, rather than cylinders, were invented by Emile Berliner in 1887, who you'll find building a helicopter on page 66. (He was an engineer and inventor of many talents!) A needle attached to a diaphragm followed the tiny lump and bumps in the grooves of the disc, or 'record', causing the diaphragm to vibrate down a metal tube, and the sound to come out – good and loud – from a horn-shaped loudspeaker. To make the needle follow the path of the groove, the record revolved on a wind-up turntable. Here was the first true record player, and it didn't need even electricity to make it

work. By 1912, Edison himself had abandoned cylinders and switched to discs too.

DISCOGRAPHY

The first discs were called 78s. They had to go around 78rpm (**revolutions** per minute) for the sound to come out at the right speed, and were very brittle and heavy. They stayed in use right up until the 1950s, by which time long-playing records (or LPs) had become popular. LPs went round at a much slower 33.33rpm and were made of vinyl. They first appeared in about 1948. Later came 'singles' – small records, usually with a single track on each side, which revolved at 45rpm. By now, record players turned the turntables and amplified the sound electrically.

GETTING IT TAPED

 The next big advance in sound recording to WOW everyone was the tape recorder. This records and plays back sound by recording electrical signals as magnetic patterns on thin, magnetic oxide-coated plastic tape. When recording, a magnetic imprint is left on the tape as it passes a 'recording head'. When playing a tape, it passes a 'reproducing head' which turns this magnetic imprint into an electrical signal. The signal is then amplified and reproduced as sound. The great thing about tapes is that you can record over them again and

again, something you can't do with records, and they don't break if you drop them! The first tape recorder was invented by a Danishman named Valdemar Poulsen in 1898. He called it a telegraphone.

SMALL IS BEAUTIFUL

For many years, tape recorders were big and bulky reel-to-reel machines, where tape unspooled from one reel onto another. Then, in the 1960s, came the far more convenient cassette recorder. The tapes for these machines came in a sealed cassette with two tiny self-contained spools. In the late 1970s and early 80s came personal stereos – tape players little bigger than the cassettes themselves.

A COMPACT SOLUTION

The 1980s also saw the Sony and Philips corporations develop the compact disc, introducing a whole new, mind-blowing level of sound quality. While record players use mechanics and tape recorders use magnetics, compact discs (often simply called CDs) use **optical** means to record and play. This breakthrough in technology has three big pluses: a whole lot of sound can be recorded onto

one small disc, the sound quality is *fab*, and the part which 'reads' the information from the disc doesn't actually touch it. Unlike a record worn down by a needle or a tape worn down by the 'heads', a CD is touched by light alone.

LASER TECHNOLOGY

Sound on a CD is recorded digitally. In other words, the audio signals are turned into a digital code made up of '0's and '1's – this digital code of the sounds then needs to be transferred to the disc. The disc has a light-sensitive base which is exposed to light from a laser which encodes the digital information – those '0's and '1's onto the spinning disc. The disc is then dunked in a chemical which etches flat spots and pits (dents) into the areas exposed to the laser beam's digitally converted sound. Clever stuff, eh?

PLAYING A CD

Instead of a record needle, a CD player plays a compact disc using a laser scanner that reflects light off the top of it. If the light hits a flat spot, this represents an '0' in the digital code. If it hits a pit, this corresponds to a '1'. The CD player then simply converts these into electrical signals that can then be reproduced and amplified as music. Today, all sounds can be recorded, mixed and played back in any order at the touch of a button. Things have come a quite a long way since Edison recorded 'Mary had a little lamb' onto a revolving foil cylinder!

PHOTOGRAPHY

1839, LACOCK ABBEY, WILTSHIRE, ENGLAND

In his darkroom, Fox Talbot continues to make history. He may not
be the first person to develop a photograph, but he's the first
person to use this method – *his* method – and the results are
remarkable. He smiles with real satisfaction as he watches the
image appear before his eyes, like some ghostly apparition. One
day, everyone will be able to take photographs, he muses …
one day …

AS IF BY MAGIC

A very early type of camera was the camera obscura,
which was usually a building as well as a camera! A
(bright) image of the view outside the building was
projected onto a flat surface in the (dark) inside, through a
convex lens. The effect was amazing. Those inside the
building, standing in the dark, could watch moving images
of the world go by! Some artists drew around these
projected images as the basis of their work so, even in an
age before true photography, a camera helped them to
make their finished paintings look so realistic. The word
'camera' actually comes from the Greek 'kamara',
meaning vault – like the dark room, or vault, of the camera
obscura.

HUMBLE BEGINNINGS

By the eighteenth century, it had been discovered that certain silver **compounds** were photosensitive – in other words, that, under certain conditions, they could create a photographic image. Using this information, the British scientists Sir Humphry Davy and Thomas Wedgwood began experiments with paper coated with silver chloride. They managed to produce basic images of silhouettes of leaves and people's profiles – faces sideways on – but these weren't proper, permanent photographs. When the paper was exposed to light, the whole print went black and the image was lost for ever.

AMAZING ADVANCES

The first true photographs weren't produced until the nineteenth century. They were taken and developed by the French physicist Joseph Nicéphore Niépce in 1822, again using silver chloride. In about 1829, he was partnered by the French painter Louis Daguerre. It was Daguerre who produced photographs on silver plates coated with a light-sensitive layer of silver iodide, in 1839. After the plates had been exposed for a few minutes to the image he was photographing, he then used **mercury vapour** to develop a positive photographic image. At first, these too went black over time, until Daguerre 'fixed' the image by coating them with a solution of salt (which stopped the silver-iodide particles being sensitive to light). This 'fixing' method was originally invented by the British inventor William Henry Fox Talbot (1800–77), who was independently working on his own method of photography, back in England. All early photographs were black and white, not colour, remember.

A SENSATION!

Daguerre held an exhibition of his photographs, which he called daguerreotypes, in Paris in 1839. (No prizes for guessing where he got the idea for that mouthful of a name from.) Thousands flocked to see these magical images. The only problem was that they were one-off positive images on a silver plate. In other words, you couldn't take copies of the same picture. This didn't stop photographers setting up portrait studios everywhere, taking daguerreotypes of eager fee-paying members of the public.

A NEGATIVE IMPROVEMENT

Fox Talbot came up with his far more practical photographic approach, also in 1839. Because Daguerre's plates held positive images, everything that was dark in the photographed scene was dark on the plate (and everything light was light). The plate itself was the finished photo. With Fox Talbot's method, however, the plate held a negative image (where everything that was dark in the original photographed scene was now light, and everything light was dark). By shining light through this negative onto light-sensitive paper, where the light got through the light patches, it turned the paper dark, and where the light was blocked out by the dark patches, it left it light. This created a positive, life-like image. And, unlike Daguerre's single positive image plate, you could use one of Fox Talbot's negatives to make as many copies of the same photo as you wanted. And what did Fox Talbot call these types of photographs? Why, talbotypes, of course!

OTHER NAMES IN PHOTOGRAPHY

Other advances in photography came from people such as French physicist Claude Félix Abel Niépce de Saint-Victor. (You may need to pause for breath after reading such a long name.) In 1847, he came up with a way of making glass-plate negatives. These produced much cleaner, sharper images than Fox Talbot's grainy paper negatives. The trouble was though, that the exposure – the length of time the camera shutter had to be open, exposing the image to the photographic plate – had to be much longer.

WET 'N' DRY

As time went on, various developments were made with both wet and dry photographic plates. The problem with wet plates was that they had to be both exposed and developed whilst they were still wet. This meant developing a photograph straight after it'd been taken. Because photographs have to be developed free from light, in darkrooms, this meant the darkroom needed to be nearby. *Very* nearby. So what happened if the photographer was miles from anywhere (on a battlefield in the American Civil War, for example)? The darkrooms came too, of course! Mobile horse-drawn darkrooms became all the rage. Fortunately, in 1878, the British photographer Charles Bennett invented a dry photographic plate – coated with a special emulsion of gelatine and silver bromide – which was very similar to the plates still used in photography today.

THE AMAZING MR MUYBRIDGE

One of the strangest people to be involved in early photography was Eadweard Muybridge. (He even changed the spelling of his name from Edward Muggeridge to the weird way you see here.) He became interested in photography when a horse breeder bet $25,000 that, when a horse was in full trot, all four of its hooves would leave the ground at the same time. (It was too fast to be sure with the naked eye.) Muybridge offered to take a series of photos to try to prove it for him. He lined one side of a racecourse with white paper (to create a clear background) and lined up a series of cameras along the other. Threads laid across the track were broken by the horse as it ran, releasing the cameras' shutters as it trotted through them. The result, in 1887, was a whole series of photos of the horse at different stages of its full trot. These included a picture that did, indeed, show the horse with all four hooves off the ground. You can find out more about Muybridge on page 118.

ROLL IN THE CHANGES

The really big advance, that suddenly made photography possible for the **masses**, was American George Eastman's invention of film-on-a-roll in 1884. This was a film made up of a long strip of paper coated with a sensitive emulsion. In 1889, he came up with the first transparent, flexible film – strips of cellulose nitrate – with the look and feel of modern film, and which easily loaded into a camera. He *also* invented a small, easy-to-carry camera: the first Kodak box camera. In 1900, he started selling the even cheaper Kodak 'box' Brownie. Now everyone was taking pictures.

HERE COMES COLOUR

Amazingly, the first colour photograph was produced as long ago as 1861, by the British physicist James Clerk Maxwell. The first colour glass plates went on the market in 1907. It wasn't until 1935 that Kodak produced its first colour film – positives that could be used to produce slides but not to make colour prints. Kodak colour negative film wasn't available until 1942 and wasn't widely used, by amateur photographers in Britain, until the mid-1960s. (Yes, when I was little, most people still took black and white photographs, and I'm not *that* old.) In 1947, Dr Edwin Land invented the Polaroid camera and instant photography was born.

LEAPS AND BOUNDS

Today, no matter the conditions, there's a camera to suit our needs. Whether it's underwater where everything seems 25 per cent bigger than it really is, or mapping whole countries – including your home – from the air, there's a special camera designed to tackle it. The Hubble Telescope takes photos of our universe. Infrared cameras make it possible to take photographs in complete darkness. Ultraviolet photography helps to prove whether documents are faked or have been tampered with (showing faint or rubbed-out words). And now more and more people are taking ordinary, everyday photos with digital cameras, which don't even have any film inside them! The image is simply stored in a digital code of '0's and '1's which, when plugged into a computer with the right software, is decoded and turned into a photograph on screen.

3-D PICTURES

One of the most remarkable recent developments in photography, however, is the hologram. A hologram is a three-dimensional photograph, which means that the object in a hologram looks different when looked at from different angles – front, left, right, above and below. A ghost in a hologram can appear to be leaping out of a wall right at you! (The word comes from the Greek 'holos', meaning 'whole' and 'gram', meaning 'message'.) The theory behind the technology to create such remarkable pictures was worked out by the British physicist Dennis Gabor as long ago as the Polaroid camera (1947), but wasn't developed until the 1960s, and wasn't wholly successful until the 1990s. Unlike an ordinary photo, holographic pictures are taken without using a lens. An object being 'photographed' for a hologram is illuminated by a laser beam of light, part of which is also reflected by a mirror or prism at a photographic plate. The shape of the object interferes with the light and it is the pattern of this interference which is recorded to create the 3-D

holographic shape – and that's putting it simply! It's a complicated process with some remarkable results.

HERE, THERE, EVERYWHERE

Today, photographs are such a part of everyday life we hardly give them a second thought. There are photographs in newspapers and magazines, on advertising billboards, bus shelter posters, in shop windows, and there are even glossy high-quality colour photos in family photo albums, or stored (without film) on our home computers. Fox Talbot wouldn't have believed his eyes …

CINEMA AND TELEVISION

26 JUNE 1926, FRITH STREET, SOHO, LONDON, ENGLAND

Scotsman John Logie Baird nervously makes the final adjustments to his prototype machine under the watchful eye of his invited guests: members of the all-important scientific society, the Royal Institution. They have come to Baird's home laboratory to see the world's first demonstration of true television. Ready at last, the expectant audience leans forward as one and ... yes ... there on the screen is a moving, human face!

THE FLICK OF A WRIST

Making pictures appear to move isn't the hardest thing in the world. If you hold this book by the spine in your left hand and flip the pages with your right, you'll see the aeroplane at the bottom of the book fly through the clouds. A similar principle was used to make moving picture machines. When the viewer turned a handle, the machine flipped through a series of still photographs, giving the impression of movement. But these machines could only be watched by one viewer at a time. (These were often

117

called 'What the Butler Saw' machines and showed naughty things a butler might have seen when peeping through a keyhole!).

A FLASH OF INSPIRATION

One of the earliest examples of a variation on this approach came from Eadweard Muybridge (who first showed up on page 113). He took a whole series of still photographs of horses trotting and galloping. He soon realized that if he was to flash one picture after another, in quick succession, he could give the impression of the horse and rider moving before our very eyes. He manged this with an invention which he called the zoopraxiscope. A glass disc, showing pictures of the horse moving in sequence, was placed in front of a light projector, and rotated between light flashes. The result was more of a horse 'running on the spot' than running off the screen, but must have been most impressive. This was years before the invention of film projectors and certainly earns Muybridge a place in early cinema history.

THE WHYS AND WHEREFORES

The reason why these methods work is because of 'persistence of vision' – in other words, our eyes keep the visual image of the picture just gone (known as the 'positive after-image') while the next picture appears, so our brains are not aware of any gaps between the pictures. Up to a point, the more pictures (or 'frames') we see a second, the smoother and less flickering the images will seem. But our eyes need 0.2 seconds to receive an image and to transmit the information to our brains, so that we're aware of what we've seen.

EARLY DAYS

Before Muybridge's zoopraxiscope was the zoetrope, a more basic machine invented in the 1830s, but working on the same principle. A series of still images were placed around the inside of an open-topped 'drum' with slits in its wall. When a person looked through the slits into the drum, and the drum was spun, the pictures whizzed past the viewer's eye quick enough to appear to be one continuous, moving image.

FIRST PROJECTIONS

By the 1870s, Frenchman Emile Reynaud had built a bigger, better zoetrope, with a reflector and a lens to enlarge the images. He even found a way of running a whole reel of images through the drum, rather than being limited to the number he could fix to the drum wall. This way, he could show hundreds of pictures – all drawings – running together to make one continuous moving 'picture show' lasting up to a quarter of an hour. He held screenings for the paying public at his Théâtre Optique in Paris. In a sense, this was almost-but-not-quite the world's first cinema. He wasn't showing photographs.

MR EDISON JOINS THE FUN

In the late 1880s, Thomas Edison took the work of Muybridge, Eastman (see page 113) and others and gave one of his **employees** the job of coming up with a machine that would record moving pictures (by quickly taking one still picture after another) and another machine to show the results. That employee was the Englishman William Dickson and, by 1891, the result was a moving picture camera called a kinetograph and a viewing machine called a kinetoscope.

FRAME BY FRAME

The camera – the kinetograph – had a motor which moved the roll of celluloid film past the lens where it was exposed to light and each single picture was taken. If the developed film was then shown on the kinetoscope projector at the same speed, the image would appear to move naturally. It was soon decided that motors made cameras heavy and difficult to lug about. These were soon replaced with much lighter and more mobile hand-cranked cameras. The most ingenious part of Dickson's invention was its **sprocket** mechanism. It was this which stopped the film in the right place for each exposure, or frame, to be taken. In these early days, different cameras used different speeds, so films had to be played back at different speeds too. And there was no sound to go with the pictures back then.

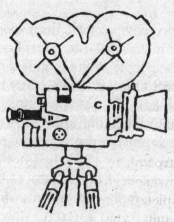

ALMOST THERE

Early moving films were often referred to as 'motion pictures' and people (particularly Americans) still speak of the 'motion picture industry' today. The word 'movies' – as in pictures-which-move – is still used to mean films. Edison built his own motion-picture studio in the grounds of his Menlo Park laboratory in 1893. Later that year, he gave a public showing of the films that he'd shot but – unlike Emile Reynaud's Paris screenings, where the Frenchman projected his moving drawings onto screens at his Théâtre Optique – only *one* member of public at a time could view the moving photographs! The viewer had to watch it through a tiny window on the front of the kinetoscope. But, crazy though this might seem today, this didn't stop kinetoscope 'viewing parlours' from cropping up in US cities in 1894.

THE BIRTH OF MODERN CINEMA

Although Edison may not have been too pleased about it, the French brothers Auguste and Louis Lumière are credited by most people as the founders of true cinema in 1895 – so much so that, in 1995, many people celebrated 100 years of cinema. (It was the Lumières who came up with the term 'cinématographe' from which we get 'cinema'.) The Lumières ran a photographic equipment factory in Lyons and, by 1895, had not only developed a better, lighter, hand-held movie camera based on the idea of Edison's kinetograph, but had also invented a way of projecting the image onto a screen. After a number of test screenings for small, invited audiences, the first public screening took place in Paris in December 1895.

ACROSS THE GLOBE

Since Edison's invention, things were moving quickly the world over. In Germany, brothers Emil and Max Skladanowsky had invented their own projector and had screened films in Berlin as early as November 1895. In Britain, Birt Acres and Robert Paul were projecting films by January 1896. Back in America, a projector called the Vitascope was developed and its inventors teamed up with Edison to go into production. What makes the Lumière brothers so special, though, is that they not only developed the camera and the projector but also made very

memorable short films to
show off their inventions –
everything from comedies
to documentaries.

BIGGER! NOISIER! IN COLOUR!

Early films had to fit on one reel and lasted about 10 to 12
minutes. Improved technology meant that films could get
longer. 'Talkies' (films with soundtracks, where you could
actually hear people speak) arrived in the 1920s. To begin
with, there were two systems. One was where the sound
was recorded onto disc, and this record was played as the
film was screened. The second was to record the
soundtrack directly onto the celluloid film strip (which is
how they are recorded today). The earliest colour films
relied on special filters being placed over the projection
lens. The first full-length colour film which didn't rely on
this approach, but used a system called two-colour
Technicolor, was made in 1922. The first film to use the
improved three-colour Technicolor was a short Walt
Disney cartoon called *The Trees and the Flowers*. The first
feature-length cartoon was also by Walt Disney: *Snow White
and the Seven Dwarfs*. Colour didn't become standard until
the 1950s, when cinema had a new rival: television.

THE SPINNING DISC

Different countries have different ideas as to who it was who invented television but the world's first commercially transmitted TV pictures were transmitted by Scottish-born John Logie Baird (1888–1946). At the heart of his invention was a mechanical device called a Nipkow Disc and the (then) latest in electronics. The disc, named after German engineer Paul Nipkow who invented it in 1884, was an upright disc – up on end, not flat like a CD – punched with a carefully ordered spiral pattern of holes. Placed in front of an object, the disc was spun. As it span, the first hole passed across the top of the object, the second passed across the object a fraction lower down, and so on. In one complete revolution, the disc's holes had 'scanned' the entire object. If a camera filmed these scanned images through the disc and electronically transmitted them to a receiver that shone light through a similar disc, Baird reasoned, then surely a picture of the object could somehow be recreated on an electronic screen at the other end? Though trained as an engineer, poor health meant that Baird had to earn his money doing odd jobs whilst experimenting and inventing in his spare time. Apart from a few lenses and the motor, his prototype was made from household objects, including an old tea chest, Nipkow Discs cut from an old hat box, a biscuit tin and a darning needle. Most of it was held together with sealing wax and string!

TV'S BASIC BEGINNINGS

In 1925, Baird was ready to put his contraption to the test. He sat a ventriloquist's dummy at one end of his London attic and prepared – fingers crossed – to transmit black and white pictures of it onto his television at the other. The image was scanned using a spinning Nipkow Disc, with a light-sensitive tube electronically recording the amount of brightness or darkness coming through each one of the particular 30 holes as it span. This information was then turned into electrical signals which were transmitted to the receiver – the television set – which contained another Nipkow Disc, this time with a lamp behind it. The signals from the light-sensitive tube in the transmitter controlled how light or dark a lamp should be, shining light through the holes of the disc. This way, it recreated how light or dark the original image of the dummy had been when scanned through the different holes –

and built up the result on a screen of 30 electronic lines, one for each hole in the disc. The result? Hey presto: flickery, black and white television pictures of the dummy. Crude, but television pictures none the less.

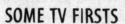

SOME TV FIRSTS

Now he needed a live, moving subject! Baird was so excited, he rushed out and found a boy called William Taynton to take the dummy's place. That afternoon, Baird repeated the experiment. The result was the world's first moving television pictures! In January 1926, Baird showed his 'television' to the public. In 1927, he sent a television picture – the signals from the light-sensitive tube to control the brightness of the lamp shining through the Nipkow Disc, down the phone line between London and Glasgow so building up a picture of shades of grey on a TV screen at the other end. A year later, he sent a picture across the Atlantic. By 1929, the BBC – the British Broadcasting *Company*, back then, not Corporation – started to transmit the world's first commercial television programmes using Baird's invention, but only occasionally! (Their main interest was radio.) By 1932, regular broadcasts were scheduled.

THE FALL AFTER THE RISE

But, however great his original achievements, John Logie Baird's success was short-lived. By 1936, his mechanical approach was outdated and replaced by less cumbersome all-electrical methods of transmitting and receiving images. (Out went the discs, in came a method of directly scanning and transmitting the electrical pattern of an image.) This was based on the Russian-born American Vladimir Zworykin's work in the USA, on both TV cameras and picture tubes. Having been the birth of television, Baird's work had already become **obsolete**.

STILL A BRILLIANT MIND

Baird may have been downhearted, but he never gave up. His contribution to TV didn't end there. In 1938, he arranged the world's first public showing of colour television in front of an audience of 3,000 at the Dominion Theatre, London. The screen was 12ft by 9ft (3.7m by

2.7m)! He also invented a system of 3-D TV, and even a method of recording TV programmes many, many, *many* years before the arrival of the video!

'INFINITY AND BEYOND!'

Today, we live in a world of hundreds of television channels, beamed across the world by **satellites** orbiting the Earth, from cables underground, or by more traditional aerial transmissions. We can record and watch films and television programmes with VCRs (video cassette recorders) and DVDs (digital video discs), and digital technology means even clearer picture and sound quality. There are even films made without cameras and projected without film! Disney's *Toy Story 2* was entirely animated on computer and, in some specially converted cinemas, could be shown on disc. Events can be beamed around the world and into our living rooms, live as they happen. Film and television have completely changed our world!

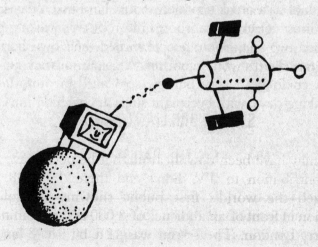

RAILWAYS

OCTOBER 1829, RAINHILL, ENGLAND

The Rainhill Trials are at an end. The competition to see who wins
the £500 prize, and whose steam locomotive will be built in
factories to pull the trains on the new Liverpool to Manchester line
are over. Five locomotives entered, only three worked well enough
to stay in the running – and there will be only one winner. Robert
Stephenson turns to his father George, on the footplate of the
Rocket. He smiles nervously. Surely, they must have won. Surely?

LEGGING IT

Before the invention of the steam locomotive, the
quickest way to get around on land was by horse. Trains
were invented before cars and planes so, before trains, what
we think of as a quick trip today could have taken days! By
far the most common transport in Europe was walking-on-
your-own-two-feet. Some people owned their own horses,
others travelled in stage coaches. A coach journey across
Britain could be a very bumpy, cold and uncomfortable
ride, taking days, with overnight stops at coaching inns.

ON THE RAILS

The first wagons to be pulled along rails were pulled by
horses, not locomotives. About 250 years ago, some miners
discovered it was much easier to get their (very heavy)

wagons of iron and coal from their mine and down to the port on rails. For the downward trip, a man rode on the back of the full wagon, controlling the speed with a brake. The horse would then pull the empty wagon, still guided by the rails, back up the hill to the mine.

GOING NOWHERE

Steam engines were also first designed for mines, but not *moving* steam engines (in other words, not locomotives). One of the earliest uses for steam was to power the pumps that took the water out of the mines, deep below the ground. (The first of these engines was built by Englishman Thomas Newcomen in 1712.) So some mines had rails, and some had static steam engines, but no one had yet thought of putting the two together and coming up with steam engines pulling wagons on rails.

FROM DANGEROUS BEGINNINGS ...

By the end of the eighteenth century, Scotsman James Watt had improved these earlier versions of static steam engines, but thought that a steam locomotive would be far too dangerous. In 1769, a Frenchman called Captain Nicholas Cugnot had WOW-ed a crowd of onlookers with a steam carriage that reached an amazing two to three miles an hour, before crashing and blowing up! The French authorities dragged away both him and what was left of his machine. Cugnot was jailed!

speed limit
2mph

WHAT, NOT WATT?

Two common **misconceptions** are that James Watt was the first to see the great possibilities in the power of steam and that George Stephenson built the first steam locomotive. Well, we've already seen that Thomas Newcomen beat Watt to it – and, in fact, a Greek inventor called Hero beat them *both* to it in Egypt over 2,000 years ago, with a steam-powered spinning ball – and we're about to see Stephenson beaten by one Richard Trevithick.

GETTING BETTER ALL THE TIME

Richard Trevithick, the son of a manager of a Cornish tin mine, built his first full-sized steam locomotive in 1801, though he had tried a few smaller models with some success before then. Instead of running on rails it ran on the road or, more to the point, it very quickly ran *off* the road – straight into some poor, unsuspecting person's house! In 1804, Trevithick was at it again. To win a bet with the owner of an iron works, he built a second locomotive – one that pulled a 10-tonne load down a ten-mile (sixteen-kilometre) track.

CATCH ME WHO CAN

Trevithick's greatest triumph was his locomotive the *Catch Me Who Can*. In 1808, he built a circular track in London and the locomotive steamed around and around it all day. The clever part was that the track was surrounded by a high wooden fence. This meant that the public could hear the noise and see the smoke from the locomotive's funnel, but the only way they could get to see it was to pay a one-shilling entrance fee – and pay it plenty of people did, even though a shilling was a lot of money in those days.

LET DOWN

What eventually caused the *Catch Me Who Can* track to close down was the same thing that stopped steam trains becoming a way of getting around in the early 1800s. The tracks weren't strong enough for the train. They kept on breaking. Wood was too weak for constant use, and the iron of the late eighteenth and early nineteenth centuries was too brittle: it snapped too easily. It was only when cast iron – an iron so strong that it had to be moulded into shapes when a molten liquid – came along that steam railways became a reality.

THE STEPHENSONS

Though not the first names in steam locomotive history, the Stephensons – George and son Robert – are two of the most famous. George Stephenson got a job in a **colliery** and one of the most important things in a colliery was moving all that coal. Like many colliery owners, George's boss, Nicholas Wood, thought that steam trains would be an excellent way of transporting such heavy loads, and George Stephenson's job was to build them. In 1825, the world's first public railway opened in England, between Stockton and Darlington. Although most of the carriages were pulled along the track by horses, sometimes a locomotive called the *Locomotion* was used. Built by George Stephenson, it could pull wagons jam-packed with hundreds of excited people (many just along for the ride), along with tonnes of cargo – all at an impressive speed of five miles an hour.

STEPHENSONS' *ROCKET*

Then, in 1829, came the Rainhill Trials. Of the four locomotives that started the competition, the *Perseverance* didn't **persevere**, because it didn't have enough power, the *Sans Pareil* (French for 'Without Equal') used up huge amounts of fuel and broke down after its eighth run, and the *Novelty* – a popular choice with the crowds – kept on grinding to a halt. Which left the Stephensons' *Rocket*. It steamed along the test track at an average speed of 14 miles an hour and was a huge success. On 15 September 1830, the Liverpool and Manchester line opened, with the

Stephensons' trains. Unfortunately,
the local MP, William
Huskisson, stepped onto
the track and was hit
and killed by the
Rocket! He was the
world's first steam railway
fatality!

> Aargh!
> 14mph!

PROBLEMS AND IMPROVEMENTS

Soon after this, improvements to steam trains and tracks
came thick and fast, and the famous engineer Isambard
Kingdom Brunel built his Great Western Railway. It wasn't
until 1892, though, that a standard gauge (width of track)
was agreed so that all trains could run on all tracks!
Before that, George Stephenson's gauge was 4 feet 3 ½
inches (1,435 mm) wide, whilst Brunel's gauge was 7 feet
(2,133 mm) wide. The one Stephenson used became
standard. Some people, meanwhile, hated everything
about the railways, which were noisy, smelly, dirty, cut
through people's land and put many stage coach
companies out of business – so it's hardly surprising, really.

OPENING UP AMERICA

On the plus side, the steam railway opened up continents.
In the past, people had set up home along rivers and roads.

Now, in countries such as the USA, people were setting up along 'railroad tracks', with telegraph lines set up alongside them. With more and more people from Europe settling in the USA, more and more people moved out west and the railways soon followed, spreading out in a network across much of this vast country. On 10 May 1869, the USA was linked from the west coast to the east when the Central Pacific and Union Pacific lines joined at a place named Promontory Point. There were big celebrations! Two of the biggest problems on early American railroads, though, were attacks from thieves (many of whom specialized in robbing trains) and from Native North Americans who didn't like the trains passing through their ever-shrinking lands.

NEW SOURCES OF POWER

Apart from the noise and the soot from the belching smoke, steam trains used up *huge* amounts of coal to heat the fire to create the steam to power the engines, so engineers and inventors looked for new ways of powering locomotives. Dr Rudolf Diesel invented what became known as the diesel engine in 1892, powered by diesel (a kind of petrol), and the discovery and harnessing of electricity made this an obvious source of power too. By the 1930s, more and more diesel and electric locomotives were being made. By the 1950s, steam-powered trains were coming to an end in Europe.

FASTER AND CLEANER

In countries with little coal, such as Switzerland, electric locomotives made a huge difference. The power usually comes from overhead cables but can also come from a third electrified rail. In Britain, most mainline trains are pulled by diesel-electric locomotives. The engine itself is diesel but it powers an electric generator which, in turn, powers electric motors which turn the wheels.

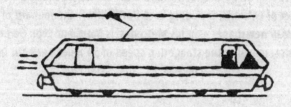

UNDERGROUND, OVERGROUND

The world's first underground railway opened in London in 1863 (but took a long, long time to grow to be anywhere near the size it is today). In 1900, this was followed by the Paris Metro in France and the New York subway in the USA. Today, we even have a train tunnel under the English Channel, joining Britain to the Continent. Meanwhile, above the streets are electric monorail trains – running on a single, central rail – and, in England in 1984, they even began running trains that float above their tracks using electromagnets. To the Stephensons, it would have seemed like magic!

CARS! CARS! CARS!

MAY 1902, BEXHILL-ON-SEA, EAST SUSSEX, ENGLAND

The 8th Earl De La Warr, in conjunction with the Automobile Club of Great Britain and Ireland, has arranged the first motor racing on British soil, with cars speeding, rattling and belching to and from Galley Hill, along the seafront. And the winner? Beating a huge number of entrants, including Lord Northcliffe – the founder of the *Daily Mail* newspaper – in his Mercedes, is Monsieur Leon Serpollet of France, reaching the staggering speed of 54 miles per hour in his steam-powered car, the *Easter Egg*!

A WHEEL, FOR STARTERS

We don't know who invented the wheel but we do know that not all societies used it to get around. The Aztecs – famous for their pyramid temples, blood sacrifices and being wiped out by their Spanish conquerors – had no carts or trucks. They had no **beasts of burden**, either, come to that. They walked or ran everywhere. In other cultures, however, people went from walking to riding to pulling carts to sitting in carts and coaches, and many went onto steam trains and, eventually, motor cars.

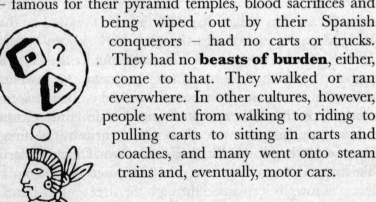

DOOMED TO FAIL

The earliest experiments with 'horseless carriages' relied on the power of the wind. A 'sailing wagon' built in the Netherlands in 1599 looked like a small sailing ship on wheels! Sailing ships had long been the fastest, biggest and most effective form of transport for thousands of years – but sails weren't so useful on land. For a start, the wind had to be blowing in the direction you wanted to drive, and the roads would have to be very smooth indeed. Like the 'windmill' and kite-powered cars, which were also suggested, the sailing wagon was of no use whatsoever!

BUILDING UP STEAM

In 1769 came Cugnot's explosive steam carriage (which you can read about on page 44) but, again, it had its serious faults. Some of the most successful early cars were made by Richard Trevithick of steam train fame so, not surprisingly, his cars were powered by steam. The first, built in 1801, got the nickname 'Captain Dick's Puffer'. The second, bigger, version of 1803 raised more than a few eyebrows as it steamed through the streets of London. Soon, passenger-carrying steam coaches were driving around the roads, but they never really caught on in

Europe. In the USA, it was a different matter. Steam coaches – and later steam cars – caught on in a big way. The *Stanley Steamer*, built in the US by twins Freelan and Francis Stanley, set a world land speed record of a staggering 121.57 miles per hour in 1906!

INTERNAL COMBUSTION ENGINE

There were many reasons for not liking steam cars, not least because you needed a furnace and boiler on board, which was a bit like driving around with a bomb! All this changed with the invention of the internal combustion engine, a remarkable invention that was to introduce motoring to the masses. Instead of steam from heated water pushing a piston down a cylinder to turn the wheels, inside an internal combustion engine a spark ignites gas (or, later, petrol vapour) to do the same. (That's what spark plugs are for, so now you know, if you didn't already, that is.) This made engines much smaller and more effective – no need for those big boilers of piping hot water or for furnaces! Few experts can agree on who actually invented the internal combustion engine, but the first person to use

one in a car was J. J. Lenior, a Belgian in Paris. His gas-powered car took two hours to travel 6 miles (10 kilometres) – an average of three miles an hour. In 1875, the Austrian Siegfried Marcus built a petrol-powered car. Surprisingly, neither Lenior nor Marcus tried to improve on their ideas. Perhaps they thought they'd made their car as good as cars could get to be. If so, they were sadly mistaken, as Mr Gottlieb Daimler and Mr Karl Benz were about to prove.

EARLY CARS

Karl Benz built the first really successful, widely purchased car in 1885. It had a lightweight frame, with two big bicycle-type wheels at the back and one at the front. He called it the Motorwagen. Unlike Benz's car, Daimler's first vehicle, built a year later, was really a carriage designed to be attached to a horse, but converted to a car, with an engine added! Ten years later, many cars still looked like carriages. The 1896 Peugeot had a cosy passenger compartment, but the driver had to sit *outside*, just as he would on a horse-drawn coach! Cars were soon all the rage and, in 1898, the Benz Viktoria was put through its paces at the London Motor Show, driving up ramps and down steps to prove just how nifty it could be!

A RUBBERY IDEA

The success of the car owes a great deal to the rubber pneumatic – air-filled – tyre. Pneumatic tyres absorb a lot of the lumps and bumps of the road, so we're not shaken

around in our cars. The American inventor Charles Goodyear discovered a process called vulcanization in 1839. This made rubber less sticky, much tougher and more elastic. In 1845, Scotsman Robert Thomson patented a basic pneumatic tyre. It was in 1888, though, that another

 Scotsman, John Boyd Dunlop, invented the rubber, pneumatic tyre similar to those used today. (Legend has it, he was experimenting with water-filled tyres, when his neighbour suggested he try air!)

ELEGANCE AND LUXURY

Gottlieb Daimler not only made Daimler cars but was soon building Mercedes with an engineer called Maybach. Right up until 1906, Mercedes were thought to be the very best cars, but then along came Mr Charles S. Rolls and Mr Henry Royce. Aristocratic car fanatic Rolls is supposed to have said to Royce, 'You make the cars, I'll sell them, and we'll call it the Rolls-Royce.' The engine of a Rolls-Royce was so quiet that it was said to purr, and so well-built that it needed very little attention. (In 1926, Daimler and Benz's companies joined together to produce Mercedes-Benz cars.)

'SO LONG AS IT'S BLACK'

Another famous phrase in the history of the car is American car-maker Henry Ford's line: 'You can have it any colour you want so long as it's black.' He was referring to his 1908 car, the Model T Ford, and the reason why each and every Model T had to be black was because it was the first car in the world to be mass-produced. Ford may not have invented the motor car, but he invented the assembly line. Each worker spent every day performing the same task on a car, in the same place on the assembly line, before it went down to the line to the next person, and so on, right down the line until the car was fully assembled, sprayed black, and ready to drive out of the factory. The Model T Fords, nicknamed 'Tin Lizzies', were cheap, reliable and an *enormous* success. In 1922, the Ford Motor Company became the first car manufacturers to make over a million cars in one year, and, by 1927 it had sold over 15 million Model Ts.

FAMILY FAVOURITES

Today, cars are accepted as an everyday part of most people's lives, but some cars stick out from all the rest. Two of the best-loved cars, with the most loyal following, are the Volkswagen Beetle and the Mini. The Volkswagen, meaning 'People's car', was first produced in Germany in 1938. This was when the Nazi dictator Adolf Hitler was in power, and he loved these cars. He even laid the foundation stone of the original Volkswagen factory! Despite its early connection with Hitler, when production of the original Beetle finally stopped in 1978, over 19.75 million had been made, which was certainly a world record. The Mini, another small car as the name suggests, was British and first rolled off the production line in 1959.

FLOPS?

Not all advances or makes of car have been rip-roaring successes. In 1958, the Ford Edsel was launched, with a pair of huge grilles on the front. What the designers had thought looked exciting and modern, the car-buying public thought looked ugly. Most Edsels stayed in the showrooms. When the company stopped producing Edsels just a year later, they'd lost $250 million! Another disaster, smaller in every way, was British inventor Sir Clive Sinclair's tiny electric car, the C5. He argued that it was economical, environmentally friendly and nippy in traffic. Many people seem to think it was just plain silly! In fact, the first electric car was invented by a Belgian in 1899 and electric cars were a common sight in the US, right up until 1930. Because they do, indeed, cause less pollution, there's renewed interest in electric vehicles – but probably not ones quite so small and low on the ground as the C5.

SAFETY

Today, safety is all-important in car design – mainly safety for those people *inside* the car. Seat belts hold the driver and passenger in place and some vehicles even have built-in child seats. Airbags automatically inflate if a car stops suddenly, or hits an object. Cars are given side-impact bars to protect occupants from side-on collisions. But now there is mounting pressure for cars to be designed to minimize harm to **pedestrians** in an accident. There are also suggestions that all cars' speeds be controlled by satellite, preventing people from breaking the speed limit.

Some specially adapted cars are designed to slow down if they are too close to the car in front, or even not to start if the driver has been drinking alcohol!

FREEDOM?

How have cars changed the world? Immeasurably. Places that were inaccessible even to the railway can be reached by car. Without having to rely on public transport and timetables, people can now go where they want, when they want and, often, considerably faster than they could on foot or horseback … except, of course, in traffic jams. In some cities, during rush hour, the average speed of a car is slower than the average speed of a horse taking the same route a hundred years ago! Horse-riders weren't stuck behind a long line of other horses, waiting at the traffic lights! Add to that the pollution, noise and road deaths, and one's reminded that – as with most inventions that have had such an impact on our world – there are disadvantages as well as advantages to living in the motor age.

AEROPLANES

17 DECEMBER 1903, KITTY HAWK, NORTH CAROLINA, USA

The two brothers have taken it in turns. Yesterday, the toss of a coin decided that Wilbur would be the first to pilot their new, improved *Flyer* but his take-off had been too steep and the plane had crashed. Today, it is Orville's turn and he's flying! He's FLYING! After covering 37 metres he's now coming in to land. He's about to successfully complete the world's first aeroplane flight!

UPS AND DOWNS

Ever since the first humans watched birds soaring through the skies, people have wanted to fly. The ancient Greek myth of Icarus tells of how he flew too close to the sun with his wings made of wax and bird feathers and how, when the wax melted in the heat, he plummeted into the sea. (His dad, Daedelus, was far more sensible and flew to safety – but this was all just make-believe, anyway.) When an English monk called Eilmer covered his arms and legs with bird feathers and jumped from the tower at Wiltshire Abbey, in the eleventh century, he didn't fly *or* die. But he did manage to break both legs.

AS HIGH AS A KITE

There are reports that, in fifth-century China, people tried strapping themselves to giant kites, with ropes firmly tethering them to the ground. This wasn't so much a way of getting about but a way of getting a good view, and there's nothing said about what happened if the wind suddenly dropped – *splat* probably.

AN IMPORTANT CONCLUSION

In the thirteenth century, *another* English monk (a chap called Roger Bacon, this time) conducted a series of studies that led him to believe that air could support a heavier-than-air craft in the same manner that water supports boats. How right he was.

HEAD IN THE CLOUDS

Then, in the early sixteenth century, along came Leonardo da Vinci, painter, architect, sculptor, musician, engineer, scientist, *inventor* and all-round, grade-one genius. He was fascinated with the idea of human flight and, amongst other things, came up with the idea for three different types of heavier-than-air aircraft. These were the ornithopter (a machine which had mechanical wings that were supposed to flap like a bird's), a helicopter – yes, I did say helicopter – and a glider (with fixed wings that would enable the pilot to coast on the air).

BACK TO THE DRAWING BOARD

These were only ever drawings on paper and, had he built them as he'd designed them, they'd never have flown, but helicopters and gliders were certainly the right idea, anyway. And, oh yes, he did invent the **propeller** *and* came up with the idea for the **parachute**. The first practical parachute, however, wasn't invented until the 1780s.

JUMP!

A Frenchman by the name of Jean Pierre Blanchard dropped a dog wearing a parachute from a great height in 1785. (I don't know what name the dog went by, as it went by.) It wasn't until eight years later – in 1793 – that Blanchard himself gave it a go and claimed to be the first person to have made a successful parachute jump. Note the word 'successful', allowing for all those people who might possibly have taken the plunge, but whom – aaaaaaaaah! – didn't live to tell the tale.

MORE THAN JUST HOT AIR

The reason why Blanchard was able to drop the dog from a great height was because he was an aeronaut: he flew in hot air balloons. The principle was simple: hot air rises, so fill a balloon 'envelope' with hot air and the balloon will rise. Attach a basket (called a gondola) to the balloon, with you inside it, and *you* will rise too. These lighter-than-air balloons were the first truly successful means of people taking to the skies. The first successfully flown balloon was built by two French brothers, Joseph and Etienne Montgolfier, and was flown across Paris in 1783 by François Pilâtre de Rozier (a scientist) and the Marquis d'Arlandes. They carried a sponge and bucket on board, just in case the craft caught fire. Suddenly, ballooning was all the rage.

SHIPS OF THE SKIES

The next step from balloons filled with hot air (which had to be continually heated from a burner positioned at an opening at the bottom of the envelope) was to airships with envelopes filled with sealed-in lighter-than-air gases. The first airship flight was piloted by Frenchman Henry Giffard in 1852, but the golden age of airships didn't begin until 1900. Amazing aircraft though they were, their frames were fragile (because they had to be so light) and could be easily damaged in storms, and the hydrogen gas inside them could be very dangerous, as in *boom*! Airships went out of fashion in 1937 after the giant Zeppelin airship, the *Hindenberg*, crashed in a mass of flames – a horrific accident which was caught on **newsreel**.

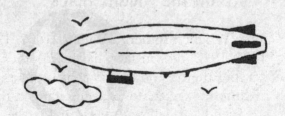

GLIDING BY

Leonardo da Vinci may have come up with the idea for a glider, but the first real glider was piloted by ... er ... by a ten-year-old boy in 1849. The glider was built by Englishman Sir George Cayley when he was 76, using the hull of an old boat for the glider's body. It was towed into the air on the end of a rope, like a giant kite. Cayley inspired the German engineer Otto Lilienthal who became the glider expert of his day. Tragically, Lilienthal died in 1896 after breaking his back in a test flight – but not before he, in turn, had inspired two American brothers who owned a number of bicycle shops: Orville and Wilbur Wright.

ON THE WRIGHT TRACK

The famous 'Wright brothers', Wilbur (1867–1948) and Orville (1871–1912) did, in fact, have two other brothers and a sister, but they're the two Wright brothers who are famous because they're the ones who changed the world. They were friends of fellow American Octave Chanute who built and flew many gliders – but they were interested in *powered* flight: flight where it was the aircraft that moved itself forward, rather than simply being carried by the air. To do this, they would need an aircraft of the right shape and weight, plus an engine turning a propeller to give the plane **lift** to take it off the ground and thrust to make it go forwards. They started off with gliders, though, building and test-flying them at the windswept sand dunes of Kitty Hawk, a fishing village in North Carolina.

REAL PLANES AT LAST

Orville and Wilbur finally decided that a powered plane couldn't simply be a glider with an engine on it. They eventually came up with the *Flyer*, with longer, narrower wings and movable tail fins, like the rudder of a ship. Next, they tested different shapes and sizes of home-made propeller, which would 'suck in' the air, pulling it (and the *Flyer*) forward and giving it lift, if everything went to plan. But was it ready to fly?

MAKING A SPLASH

On 8 December 1903, Professor Samuel Langley, head of the famous Smithsonian Institution in America, launched his own aircraft, *Great Aerodrome*, for the second time. Fired from a catapult on top of a specially converted houseboat on the Potomac River, it fell straight into the water . . . just as it had the first time. Failure though it was, the Wright brothers knew that the race was now on to be the first to fly. And, on 17 December 1903, they were. The *Flyer* worked – their whole design of wing shape, hull and propeller came together to get a person off the ground and moving through the air! After the world's first flight of a piloted and powered heavier-than-air machine, by Wilbur, which lasted no more than 12 seconds, the brothers had three more flights that day. The furthest was 260 metres in 59 seconds.

ONWARDS AND UPWARDS

From these humble beginnings, international air travel was born. Planes quickly became bigger, better, faster and more powerful. Then came the biggest advance in **aviation** since the Wright brothers: the invention of the jet engine by Englishman,
Sir Frank Whittle,
patented
in 1930.
Instead of air
being 'sucked'
through a
plane's propellers,
it could be sucked
through fan-like engines,
pulling bigger planes at far faster
speeds. In 1976, Concorde went into
service as the world's first supersonic
passenger plane – travelling faster than the
speed of sound. The helicopter, meanwhile,
had become a reality too. A great many people
had a go at building one at the beginning of the twentieth century, but the Americans Emile Berliner and his son Henry built a helicopter which was probably the first aircraft supported by its powered **rotors** to make a genuine, controlled flight. The first truly, 100 per cent successful helicopter was a machine with twin rotors built by the German engineer Heinrich Focke and flown in 1936. Three years later, Russian-born American Igor Sikorsky flew a practical single-rotor helicopter. Helicopters were here to stay.

BY THE SEAT OF THE PANTS

In flight, safety is everything and the ejection seat, invented by Sir James Martin in the 1940s, still saves pilots' lives today. A pull-handle releases the glass canopy above the pilot's head and ejects the seat through the opening. Small parachutes slow the seat down, then a secondary, larger, parachute opens, pulling the pilot free from the seat and carrying him to the ground. This is an example of a brilliantly simple idea amazingly executed.

AMAZING ADVANCES

Today, people not only fly through the skies but also in space. Although it takes off by being given a piggyback by a rocket, the space shuttle looks and lands like an ordinary fixed-wing plane. Now, nowhere in the world is more than 24 hours away. Many people also take flying as a passenger in a jumbo jet for granted. The jumbo – real name Boeing 747 – is the largest plane in the world. Amazingly, one of its wings is almost the distance of the first flight of the Wright brothers' *Flyer*!

THE GUN

26 OCTOBER 1881, O.K. CORRAL, TOMBSTONE, ARIZONA, USA

Doc Holliday, Wyatt Earp and his two brothers face the Clanton gang of suspected cattle rustlers at the start of what is to become one of the most famous gunfights in history: the gunfight at the O.K. Corral. Three of the Clantons won't live to see another day, two of the Earps will be wounded. Doc Holliday and Wyatt Earp will pass into legend ...

HUNTER GATHERERS

The first weapons used by humans – back in the days of prehistory – were probably rocks and large sticks. You can do a lot of damage with a big rock, but I don't recommend you try it. Later came clubs, spears, axes and bows and arrows. In the early days, most weapons were

probably used to hunt animals, not for attacking each other.

TRUE CRAFTSMANSHIP

About 11,000 years ago, people settled down to become the first farmers (rather than being constantly on the move, hunting animals and gathering berries) and had time to concentrate on improving their weapons. The heads of early spears and arrows were made from flint but, later, copper and bronze was used. To begin with, axes and spears were 'tanged' – the pointy heads were bound to the handles or hafts with leather strips or string. By the end of the **Bronze Age**, however, they were fitted in place with proper sockets. By the **Iron Age**, weapons were skilfully made and, often, beautifully decorated. The more important you were, the grander your sword, dagger, helmet and shield.

DIFFERENT TIMESCALES

What type of weapons people used and when depended very much on what part of the world you came from. As long ago as *c.*1485BC – that's about 3,485 years ago – Egyptians were riding two-wheeled war chariots, for example. There was nothing similar going on in Europe at the time. In *c.*500BC – yup, about 2,500 years ago – the ancient Greeks had triple-decker warships! In 600 – still 1,400 years ago – the Byzantine navy used 'Greek fire', a terrifying flaming liquid fired from tubes!

THE MIGHT OF THE ROMANS

The ancient Romans – whose massive empire was at its height under Emperor Trajan (AD98–117) – had some very impressive weapons and tactics too. Their soldiers wore uniforms with plenty of flexible body armour and helmets and either a *gladius* short-sword if on horseback, or a *pugio* dagger if on foot. They also carried spears. Bigger weapons included siege towers – wooden towers on wheels which, packed with soldiers, could be pushed against the wall of an enemy's defences, allowing the Romans to swarm out and over the top. They had battering rams (to knock down gates) and wooden-framed catapult machines too. These catapults could fire stones a distance of 30 metres (92 ft)!

VIKING ATTACK!

Later came the **Dark Ages**, the time of the Vikings and Saxons in Europe where, in many ways, things seemed much more primitive than what had gone before. The Vikings were an impressively fierce warrior people (though they rarely, if *ever*, had horns on their helmets, whatever anyone might tell you). They had huge double-edged swords and frightening battleaxes, and must have been a terrifying sight as they approached your shore in a Viking longboat, complete with a figurehead carved like a

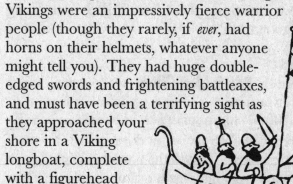

frightening beast. Only important Saxons had swords. Most foot soldiers had much more basic weapons. King Harold's Saxon army, who faced the invading William the Conqueror's Norman army at the Battle of Hastings in 1066, included many peasants armed with nothing more than rocks and sticks (as in prehistoric times)!

NEW AND IMPROVED

The big advance in weapons came in the Middle Ages in Europe, with the incredible improvement on the age-old idea of the bow and arrow. Now there was the longbow and the crossbow. The longbow remained more like the traditional bow and arrow but was almost as tall as the **archer** who fired it, and used steel-tipped arrows. It could kill an enemy soldier at 91 metres (100 yards). The crossbow was more of a machine. Imagine a bow on its side, with a wooden shaft running down the middle where the arrow goes. When the bowstring is pulled back, it's held in place on the shaft and an arrow slipped into position. Aim, pull the trigger, and the arrow fires. It was impressive and lethal, and something the Chinese had been using since as long ago as *c.*400BC!

PROS AND CONS

A crossbow's arrow could travel far greater distances than a longbow's arrow, and do far more damage . . . but they took much longer to load. To pull the bowstring tight, some crossbows needed special winding mechanisms! The reason why so many castles had cross-shaped slit windows was so that both longbows and crossbows could be used. A longbow could be fired from the vertical slit and a crossbow from the horizontal.

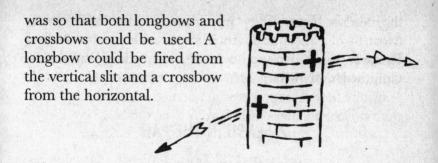

'BOOM!'

The biggest change in European weaponry, though, was undoubtedly the introduction of gunpowder: an explosive mixture of potassium nitrate, charcoal and sulphur. This was the first explosive known to humans. A barrel on its own might blow a hole in a wall ... in the barrel of a weapon it could fire even more deadly **projectiles**! The original recipe for gunpowder was probably concocted in China, with the earliest-known formula published there in 1045. At that time, the Chinese were more interested in using it to make firecrackers rather than weapons, though they were using 'war rockets' in 1232. The formula for gunpowder can be found in the writings of the thirteenth-century English monk Roger Bacon (the same Roger Bacon who came up with some brilliant thoughts on aeroplanes on page 145), and it was probably introduced to the west via the Middle East. The Swedish chemist Alfred Nobel, inventor of dynamite in 1867 and founder of the **Nobel Prizes**, went on to invent ballistite, a smokeless gunpowder, in 1889.

A FLASH IN THE PAN

By 1334, gunpowder was being produced on a large scale in England, and in Germany by 1340. The first, most basic, cannon was the bombard. It fired very large stone balls and must have seemed the ultimate weapon in fourteenth-century European warfare – like nothing seen before. By c.1400 matchlock weapons were invented, where the pulling of a trigger didn't fire an arrow but struck a match, which then ignited the 'flash' in the pan of the gun, which, in turn, lit the gunpowder in the barrel, which fired the 'shot' (pellets) . . . at least, that was the idea, but matchlocks weren't terribly reliable. So much could go wrong: the match might not strike, or it might just light the flash in the pan. (And yes, that's where the phrase comes from.) Worse than that, the pistols sometimes exploded.

GUNS! GUNS! GUNS!

By 1458, Leonardo da Vinci (yes, him again) was sketching ideas for multi-barrelled machine guns! (A man called Maxim didn't invent the first effective machine-gun until 1883. It fired 500 bullets per minute.) In 1593 came the first flintlock pistol, though the safest, and most reliable, version was probably invented by the Frenchman Martin Le Bourgeoys in the 1620s. Flintlocks remained popular right up until the 1830s. Instead of the match, the flash was lit by the spark of striking flints. With such pistols, the gunpowder and shot had to be poured down the barrel and tamped into place with a ramrod. Special flintlocks included grenade launches. Grenades aren't a modern invention. How do you think the grenadiers originally got their name?

THE SOUND OF PERCUSSION

In 1807, percussion lock pistols were invented. They fired more quickly and more safely, and it didn't matter so much if they were wet. In early percussion weapons, a small cap of detonator exploded when hit by the gun's hammer, sending a jet of flame to the powder, which fired the ball. Later, the cap, powder and ball were combined to create a single cartridge. Then, in 1836, Samuel Colt patented his revolver: percussion-fired, with a five-chamber cylinder which revolved automatically to line up the next bullet with the barrel. (The first revolver had been invented in 1818, but it was a flintlock with a chamber that had to be turned by hand.) By 1847, the Colt was in general use – this was the same year that the deadly explosive nitroglycerine was discovered.

BOMBS!

The first real air raid – bombing from the air – was in 1915 when Zeppelin airships dropped bombs on London. The first tanks were in action in 1916, with the British Mark 1 on the battlefield of the Somme in France. A year later, the world's first guided missile was launched. Unlike today's hi-tech devices, it was a biplane on autopilot, packed with 136 kg (300 lb) of explosives!

MORE AND MORE FIREPOWER

Since then, everything has snowballed. After the revolver came the semi-automatic – a self-loading handgun firing a shot at the pull of the trigger, and the automatic – a self-loader which fires repeatedly once the trigger is pulled. Both rely on a magazine full of cartridges clipped into the handle of the weapon. Today, military personnel, with their armoured cars, tanks, ships and planes, are armed to the teeth! With the discovery of the power of the atom – which you can read all about in *Discoveries* the first part of this book – came atomic weapons. There was the A-Bomb, the H-bomb, and then intercontinental ballistic missiles: weapons powerful enough to destroy Earth and everyone on it. Whether you see that as an advance on using big rocks and sticks is, of course, a matter of opinion, but guns and the weapons that followed have undeniably changed our lives. For those of us living in a world of guns, it's virtually impossible to imagine what it would be like without them. There would probably have been far fewer wars and, what wars there still would have been would certainly have resulted in far fewer deaths.

160

PRINTING

1455, MAINZ, GERMANY

Johann Gutenberg carefully lifts out the piece of paper from his printing press, the ink still wet. His hands shake slightly. He is holding the final page of his 1,282-page book. He has used over 400,000 separate letters to create the very first printed Bible in the world.

THE BIRTH OF HISTORY

The birth of writing was the birth of history, literally. Anything that happened before writing is known as prehistory, which is where we get the word 'prehistoric' from. The earliest form of record-keeping was probably nicks out of a stick or bone, one nick representing one animal owned. True writing developed in a place called Sumer (which is in what is now Iraq) round about 5,500 years ago, and a little later in ancient Egypt. Very few people in these societies could read or write. In Egypt, this was the special job of people called scribes. It took them about twelve years to learn all they needed to know.

IMPRESSIVE BEGINNINGS

Early forms of writing weren't written on paper but carved into wax tablets or onto stone monuments or buildings. An ancient library of wax tablets was found in Elba, Iraq. (Yup, they even had libraries back then . . . but not with any

LIBRARY

of my books in them.) The earliest forms of printing are ancient too. Stamps – not the things you lick 'n' stick but the things you stamp with – are probably the earliest examples, and were used in Babylonia. A design or symbol would be cut into stone and then used as a signet to leave an impression in clay as a seal, or rubbed with an early form of ink (made from mud or natural pigment) and stamped to leave a mark. Some stamp or **signet** stones were set in rings, worn by important people who used them as their signatures.

HANDMADE

For a long, long time books throughout the world were, however, written by hand. If you wanted more than one copy of a book, it had to be copied out, letter for letter. This didn't stop the ancient Romans publishing over 5,000 copies of the same book – each one having been copied out by one of a group of unpaid, but **literate**, slaves! Some of the most famous hand-written books which survive today, however, were written in medieval monasteries. These are called illuminated manuscripts.

EAST IS EAST

Printing in the East and printing in the West developed in different ways and different speeds. This was at a time when East and West were cut off from one another, so it wasn't so easy to pinch ideas and inventions off each other! The first form of printing to develop in China was for printing pictures and designs onto clothing in the 1st century AD. By the 2nd century AD, these skills had been used to print text – words – too.

ON THE BLOCK

The method the Chinese used was block printing, where whole pages or words were carved into a piece of wood, back to front, so, when pressed onto paper, they would come out the right way around. In AD972, the sacred Buddhist scriptures, called the *Tipitaka*, was printed using wooden blocks. It was more than a staggering 130,000 pages long!

MOVABLE TYPE

The printing process which was to revolutionize the West in the fifteenth century – some 1,300 years later – was actually invented by a Chinaman in the second century. Rather than carving out a whole page of type on a single block, why not use movable type, where you could rearrange the characters to make up different words and sentences and use them again and again, he argued? The problem was that, unlike English – where you'd only need

an alphabet of 26 letters, the numerals 0 to 9, and a handful of punctuation marks to make up all the words, numbers and sentences you'd ever need – the Chinese language uses up to 40,000 separate characters! It's not surprising that the invention proved unpopular in China and was soon dropped.

PAPER! PAPER!

An important part of the printing process was what you printed *on*. In the West, people wrote on papyrus (made of woven reeds) and vellum (a tissue from the hides of skinned animals). Papyrus was too fragile to print on and vellum too expensive. When the Chinese invented paper, in about AD105, they'd come up with a tough, cheap alternative to both. Paper could be made from bark, straw, leaves and even rags!

LATER, IN THE WEST

The invention of paper didn't reach the West until the twelfth century, and didn't really spread throughout Europe until two hundred years later. By the middle of the fifteenth century, though, there was paper, paper everywhere – and along came Johann Gutenberg of Mainz, in Germany. Gutenberg is said to have invented his printing press in 1450 and to have started work on the Gutenberg Bible in 1455. (Other Western countries have since laid claim to *their* inventing movable type before

Gutenberg but, even if that's true, they hadn't made such a good job of it as Gutenberg. His Bible – copies of which still survive today – are so beautiful that they look very like genuine, hand-written and hand-drawn illuminated manuscripts.) In next to no time, printing presses were springing up everywhere. William Caxton set up his printing press in England in 1476 and many Britons imagine that it was Caxton who invented this method of printing. How wrong they are – and you know better.

THE EARLY PRESSES

The Chinese had simply hand-pressed their wooden blocks of type, covered with water-based paint, onto paper. Western printers always used more permanent, oil-based paint, and built presses that could screw down the type hard and flat onto the paper. (The paper was placed on a 'bed' and the type was pressed down onto it with the 'platen'.) This was a slow business. Only one side of a page could be printed at a time, and the platen had to be

screwed up and down between each printing. In the seventeenth century, someone had the bright idea of adding springs so that the platen could be raised and lowered much faster. Iron presses were introduced in about 1800. Up until then, all presses had been wooden. Now levers replaced the huge screws that pressed the platen against the bed. These presses were much bigger, so many pages could be printed onto one huge sheet of paper, which was then folded and cut into the pages of a book.

LEAPS AND BOUNDS

Early Western printing presses were mostly used for religious or worthy works. As printing got cheaper, thousands of pamphlets were printed, putting forward every political point of view under the sun. More and more newspapers cropped up, requiring bigger and bigger machines. In the nineteenth century, steam-powered presses appeared, along with presses that could print *both* sides of the paper at once. In 1863, the American inventor William A. Bullock patented the first newspaper press to print from enormous rolls of paper rather than flat sheets. By 1871, another American, Richard March Hoe, had invented the continuous roll press which could print a staggering 18,000 newspapers an hour!

HOT METAL

The invention of the Linotype typesetting machine in 1886 and the commercial use of Monotype typesetting machines in the 1890s really speeded up the setting of the metal type – putting the correct letters in place ready for the printing presses. The Linotype could cast whole lines of type at once, the Monotype produced single letters. The advantage of this second method was that the letters could used again and again, and at very high speed. Then, in the 1950s, along came the first phototypesetting machines. Instead of setting actual type in metal, they produced photographic negatives of the type which could then, like ordinary photography, be used to make plates but, in this case, **lithographic plates**. By the 1960s, photo-typesetting pretty much had done away with a printing process that had been perfectly good for about 500 years.

COMPUTER MAGIC

Then, suddenly, the whole printing world was turned upside down *again*. This time by the invention of computers. Computers can do everything from setting type to scanning and retouching photographs, putting everything together on a single piece of film or even straight onto a printing plate. Late twentieth-century advances in desktop publishing meant that it was even possible for people to print out high-quality documents from their own personal PCs at home. With the introduction of the internet and e-mail, the need to print out so much information onto paper has been greatly reduced. Nowadays there are many newspapers and magazine that don't actually exist on paper, but simply on-line, on screen. We've come a long, long way since Gutenberg and the Chinese. Today, a single copy of a Sunday newspaper contains more words and information than the average fourteenth-, fifteenth-, sixteenth- or even seventeenth-century person had access to in their lives.

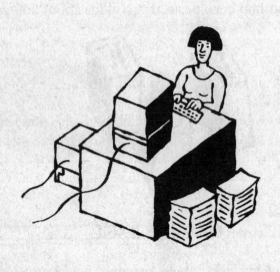

THE COMPUTER

DATE: CLASSIFIED, BLETCHLEY PARK, ENGLAND

World War II is over and the work at Bletchley Park, home to Project X, is at an end too. On the orders of the prime minister, Winston Churchill, all evidence of the **classified** operations carried out here are being destroyed. And that includes the world's first programmable computer – a computer so top-secret that the rest of the world won't hear about it until 1974, almost thirty years later!

CALCULATING MACHINES

In the days before PCs, e-mail and the internet, a computer's main function was to compute (work out) numbers and data – hence the name. For that reason, you could argue that the abacus (where different beads on a frame represent tens, units, hundreds and so on) is an early computer; *very* early, in fact. They've been around for 5,000 years (since 3000BC). But that's not a proper computer though, is it? Is it? Then what about the German William Schickard's 'calculator clock' of

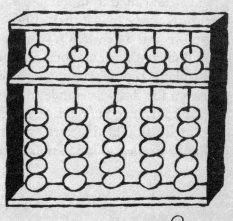

1623? He claimed it could multiply any two six-digit numbers together, which is more than my calculator can do – there's no room in the display window for the answer. Schickard's calculator clock was reconstructed in 1960, and it worked. Then, in 1642, there was Frenchman Blaise Pascal's 'Pascaline' machine – which wasn't such a success because it kept on jamming. (This probably pleased a lot of locals, by the way. Pascal had built it to help his dad work out how much money he needed to take off people, in his job as a tax collector!) In 1673, another German, this time one Gottfreid Leibniz, built a highly successful calculating machine that not only multiplied, added and subtracted but divided too – could that be seen as an early computer?

BABBAGE, THE MAIN MAN

Whatever the answer, most experts agree – yes, *agree* – that one person is 'father of the computer' and that person was Englishman Charles Babbage (1792–1871). Babbage had a brilliant mind. The British government actually gave him £17,000 to build a very complicated mechanical calculator which he called a 'difference engine'. That was a *very* big sum of money back then. But, after ten years, the money ran out and they wouldn't give him any more. Although all of Babbage's calculations had been right, his mechanical calculator kept on coming up with the wrong answers. The reason for this was simple: nineteenth century technology wasn't advanced enough to build the kinds of machine he wanted to build. He was even having to invent the tools that he needed to use to make certain parts of the 'engine'!

ANOTHER BRILLIANT FAILURE

Abandoning his 'difference engine', Babbage invented his 'analytical engine' in 1833. This was an even more brilliant invention, but one he couldn't even start to build, let alone finish! It was a machine which could be programmed to do lots of different functions, which could store the results ('remember' them) and then print them out on paper – if only he could actually build one! What Babbage was trying to create was a machine that does exactly what electronic computers do today. He was, sadly, a genius who got nowhere.

ANOTHER WORLD FIRST

Babbage was ably assisted by Ada Byron, Countess of Lovelace (**aka** Lady Ada Lovelace), another person with an amazing mind. Lady Ada was the world's first true computer programmer! Methods she worked out for programming Babbage's 'analytical engine' were early versions of the language actually used in modern computers, and involved cards punched with a series of holes. Hole-punch cards and, later, strips were to become a vital part in computers (but were originally used to programme looms to weave certain patterns). And don't

forget the secret of how the Pianola played its tunes on page 101. Sadly, Babbage spent 37 years working on the 'analytical engine' with no end result, and Lady Ada – a gambler – died penniless. In 1991 the Science Museum in London built a copy of the difference engine using modern, machine-tooled components, in time for the 200th anniversary of Babbage's birth in 1792. It contained over 4,000 parts, weighed over 3 tonnes and worked *perfectly*.

ON THE HOLE

In 1886, American inventor Herman Hollerith devised a successful method of recording information using the hole-punch card method, and building a machine to 'read' them. Information from the 1890 US **census** was recorded onto hole-punch cards, and his tabulating machines could then analyse the statistics. Hollerith formed a company in 1896 with the snappy title of the Computing-Tabulating-Recording Company. It grew and grew and grew and, in 1924, changed its name to the International Business Machines Corporation – or IBM, for short.

COMPUTER GIANTS

Throughout most of its existence, IBM has been the biggest computer corporation in the world. Its first chairperson was a man called Thomas Watson (though not, as far as I'm aware, the same Thomas Watson who was shouted at by Alexander Graham Bell back on page 92).

As far as Watson concerned, the most important thing his employees could do was to *think*.

THE BREAKTHROUGH

1941 saw the construction of the world's first all-electric programmable computer: Colossus. Well, in fact, only very few people actually *saw* the construction of the machine, let alone the finished result. Designed and built by Englishman
Tommy Flowers,
one of a team at
Bletchley Park,
Woking, under
Alan Turing –
brilliant
mathematician,
codebreaker and
pioneer of
computer theory
– Colossus was
top, top, *top* secret

and built to crack the Nazi's codes in World War II. In early tests, it could read information off paper tape optically at speeds of up to 60 miles of tape an hour! Colossus was very large, and it relied on electrical **valves**, so got very hot. The computer room was a popular place to work in during the cold winters, but not in hot summers. It was also an excellent place for drying clothes!

SAYING NOTHING

Even after the war, Colossus remained a secret under Britain's **Official Secrets Act**. As late as 1973, a US judge declared – as part of a legal case over a patent – that a computer, completed in 1942 by an American named Atanasoff, was the first – unaware of Tommy Flowers's remarkable achievement. Yet no one could tell the judge that he was wrong! Flowers was a telephone engineer by trade and, after the war, he was unable to tell anyone about his amazing invention and went back to his old job! The secret only came to light in a book published in 1974, which broke the Official Secrets Act.

INCREDIBLE SHRINKING MACHINES

The first all-purpose computer was built from 1943 to 1945 at the University of Pennsylvania in the US and is called ENIAC (short for Electronic Numerical Integrator And Computer). Unlike Colossus, it was designed to do lots of different tasks. Soon, other people were building computers and, because they also relied on valves, these had to be huge too. Then, in 1947, the transistor was invented. It was developed by three Americans – Brattain, Bardeen and Schockley – and had such a big impact on everything from radios to computers that it won them the Nobel Prize for Physics in 1956. Why? Because a tiny transistor did the work of large, easily breakable and heat-creating valves.

CHIPS WITH EVERYTHING

The next big leap came when transistors were, in turn, replaced by **silicon chips** – sometimes called microchips because they're so microscopically small – in 1969. This was really the beginning of what we think of as computers today. By 1975, the Altair, the first personal computer, went on sale – not that you'd recognize it as one. First, you had to build it yourself, as it came as a kit! Secondly, it didn't have a screen! Thirdly, there was no '**qwerty**' keyboard! It was all about flicking switches and flashing lights. A version of the BASIC computer-programming language was developed for the Altair by two Harvard University students: Paul Allen and Bill Gates.

A FLOOD OF CHANGES

In 1980, a company called Acorn manufactured BBC computers for the BBC (British Broadcasting Corporation) to go with a programme about computers. The BBC thought they might manage to sell as many as 10,000 computers. In fact, they sold over a million. Next came Sir Clive Sinclair's Sinclair Spectrum computer, another big hit, especially because it could generate colour graphics on screen. Then, in 1981, came IBM's PC which had the basic look that modern computer **hardware** has today. 1984 saw the Apple company build their Macintosh computer. Apple Macs were easier to use than IBM's PC. They had easy-to-follow icons on screen, and the user could do much less typing-in of commands. In 1985, IBM brought in a similar look, using Windows software designed by Microsoft. This was a company set up by Bill Gates and

Paul Allen, who'd dropped out of Harvard by now, with the idea of working towards 'a computer on every desk and in every home'. Today, most computers in the world use Windows and Bill Gates is one of the richest men in the world.

AND NOW?

Computers have changed beyond recognition. A laptop computer, smaller than a briefcase, can perform operations in minutes that an old-fashioned computer, the size of a room, took days to do! Back in 1943, Thomas Watson of IBM didn't think there'd be a need for more than five computers in the whole world. Today, they're in millions of people's homes and some people are even doing their weekly shopping on them! There are computers that can talk, using speech synthesis. There are computers that can listen, using voice recognition.

THE WORLD WIDE WEB

We can't discuss the invention of computers without mentioning the invention of the internet. As early as the 1960s, computers at military bases across the US were linked to each other, in a network. In the 1970s, universities across the US networked their computers and soon other universities in other countries were doing it too. By the 1980s, computers from different countries were networked to each other and the internet was born, but computer users needed to have a specific computer's address before being able to communicate with it.

Then, in the 1990s, Tim Berners-Lee, an employee of a Swiss company called CERN, invented the world's first browser – a program which, once given a name or topic to look for, searched the network for it. Now anyone could surf the World Wide Web! Today, there are almost forty million users.

THEY'RE EVERYWHERE!

Computers are remarkable in just how quickly they've changed the way we can do just about everything. Want to get out some money? Use a cashpoint machine. Want to find a book in the library? Use the on-screen catalogue. Want to know the speed a race was run? Check the electronic timekeeper. Want to guide a missile? Pilot a plane? Set the central heating controls? Book a holiday? Monitor a patient's blood-flow and heartbeat? Regulate their drugs? Record a song? Store a photo? There are computers to do all of these things and more. And will there really soon be a new breed of computers that can think for themselves, like we do? Perhaps you should ask one. Nicely.

IDEAS
that Changed the World

For all the good who died young

IDEAS!

Imagine a world where no one's come up with the idea of money, so we have to barter for everything – where you were given this book in exchange for a bag of apples or a box of nails. Imagine a world without religions, so there won't have been any Crusades or Inquisitions but there won't have been any spiritual guidance and comfort for billions, either. There are so many things that we accept as everyday parts of our lives that it's easy to forget that they're big ideas put into practice . . . and that, in some cases, people gave their lives to turn these ideas into a reality. In this *WOW!* book we take a look at some of the ideas that changed the way we live or think about the world today. There's the idea that people shouldn't be judged by the colour of their skin. There's the idea that women should have the vote as well as men. There's the idea that everything should be shared equally amongst everyone. And what of the world-changing ideas of the future? Who knows? Perhaps you already have the glimmering of a great idea forming in your mind.

PHILIP ARDAGH
2000

COMMUNISM

30 DECEMBER 1922, MOSCOW, RUSSIA

Comrade Vladimir Ilyich Lenin's health is poor and his body
weakened – following an attempt to assassinate him some four
years earlier – but nothing can take away the feeling of triumph
and accomplishment that today brings. Today, after the October
Revolution of 1917 and the defeat of the anti-Communist 'White
Russians' in 1920, Lenin has lived to see the creation of the
Soviet Union – a mighty Communist empire!

THE IDEA

The *idea* of Communism and how it works in practice are
two very different things. The idea of Communism is to
be as fair as possible. A Communist society would be a
society where all the natural resources – coal, gas, gold and
diamonds, for example – belong to the people, along with
all the mines and equipment needed to extract them. No
one would pay lighting or water bills. All jobs would be
shared out equally amongst the people, based on their
abilities, and all benefits would be given to people
according to their needs. No one would own their own
home. Society would build and provide homes for
everyone. Once such a society was up and running, there'd
be no need for government or rulers, so everyone would be
equal. And you can't get much fairer than that.

THE REALITY

The reality was, of course, very different from the word go, not least because no societies – or very, very few – are built from scratch. In other words, to achieve Communism you need revolution. Because *private* property needs to become *public* property – belonging to all people – it needs to be taken away from the original owners . . . something which most of them are likely to be unhappy about! And such revolutions need to be organized and led and, once the revolution is won, these leaders usually want to keep on leading for fear that, if they don't, others (with different ideas) will. It's all very well saying that everything belongs to everyone and that 'all property is theft', but someone needs to make sure that it stays that way. So there needs to be a police force and an army, and officials to check that the right people are receiving the right benefits and so on and so on. So, in a society where everyone is supposed to be equal, there will still be those with more power and importance than others – and this is why many argue that Communism in *practice* is doomed.

THE ROOTS OF THE IDEA

The idea of an ideal society being one where the people (the society itself rather than individuals) owned everything and decided everything goes back to Ancient Greece and the writings of people such as Plato. The philosopher Plato (*c.*423BC–347BC) wrote a series of books called the *Republic*, based on the whole matter of justice. This discussed everything from 'what is an individual?' to 'what is the state, or society?'. He saw the ideal state as being made up of three distinct classes: the ruling classes (the wise 'philosopher-kings'), the military classes (the courageous soldiers and sailors) and the merchant classes (the **temperate** traders, creating a healthy economy). What was different about his state, though, was that you weren't born into a particular class. Just because you were the child of a philosopher-king didn't mean that you'd grow up to govern. Just because your dad was a general didn't guarantee you a cushy job in the army. No. Everyone would receive exactly the same education until that person reached a level of education where their ability and interest could take them no further. So the class you belonged to depended on when you stopped your education. Being a philosopher-king required the sharpest mind and the most knowledge so, logically, these would be the pupils who carried on their education right up to the end of the process. For such a republic to work, Plato reasoned, none of the classes must put pressure on any of the others so, as well as wisdom, courage and temperance there had to be justice too. Although the rigid 'three classes' system might not appeal to later Communists, the idea of the same education and opportunities for all most definitely did.

COMMUNAL LIVING

A number of attempts at creating sharing societies, where people treated each other more equally, came about as a result of religion. These weren't whole countries but small communes (mini-communities) where people lived together on the basis that the good of the commune was more important than the comfort of any one individual. Prime examples of such communes are Christian monasteries, priories and nunneries which spread right across Europe in the Middle Ages. Later, in the sixteenth and seventeenth centuries, when **Protestant** Christians were persecuted, this led to them setting up their own communes – including in places such as America, far away from their persecutors.

THE NINETEENTH CENTURY

In the nineteenth century a number of cooperative movements flourished, where members benefited from goods and services shared fairly amongst them. However, most members of such groups still lived in mainstream society. One of the most successful experiments in communal living was the Oneida Community, set up in Oneida, New York State in the US in 1848. It'd originally been founded by John Humphrey Noyes in Vermont back in the 1830s, based on the principle that, to be close to God, you must give up all personal possessions and ties – including such things as marriage – and live together in a sharing community. This wasn't too popular with some of the locals, hence the move to New York. A large community, it ran a number of different industries as well as farms and was controlled by a committee. Unusually, women had exactly the same rights as men, and children were raised by the community as a whole. In the end, the original principles of the Oneida Community were lost and, in 1880, the business side of it became a company.

KARL MARX

True Communism – or at least the theory of it – arrived in the form of *The Communist Manifesto* written by Karl Marx (including ideas of fellow Communist Fredrich Engels) and published in London in 1848. This was a declaration of the aims of a secret group calling themselves the Communist League, founded the year before and made up of German workers and intellectuals who'd been forced into **exile** because of their aims. The introduction contains a warning. 'A spectre is haunting Europe,' it states. 'The spectre of Communism.' Much of the Manifesto discusses the 'class struggle' between what Marx saw as the two main classes: the **capitalists** and the working classes. He called these the 'ruling bourgeoisie' and the 'downtrodden proletariat'. The argument was that the bourgeois capitalists became rich at the expense of the working classes who would eventually rise up against them, and that the Communists would be the true saviours of the working classes. After the inevitable revolution, the working classes would also be the ruling classes – so there would be no such thing as class. The main force behind the Communist Manifesto can best be summed up in its call for action: 'Workers of the world, unite!'

THE LEGACY OF MARX

The Communist League was disbanded in 1852 and, when Karl Marx died in 1883 – having written a number of other important works, including *Das Kapital* – his mark on the world wasn't that great – but his time would come. It was *after* his death that Marx's words had their greatest influence. His particular branch of Communism became known as Marxism and was the basis of Bolshevism: Marx's theories as developed by the Russian leader Lenin. There were two revolutions in Russia in 1917; in March and in November. The March revolution saw the overthrow of the Tsar (the Russian monarch) and the setting up of a **republic**. The revolution in November saw Lenin and his Bolshevik Communists come to power. (The revolution in November is sometimes referred to as the 'October Revolution' because, at the time, the Russians were using an old calendar system which was thirteen days behind the Western world, putting events in 'their' October.) This second revolution was bloodless. The civil war between the Bolsheviks and anti-Bolsheviks which followed wasn't. Many died on either side, but the Communists were finally victorious. Russia and the soon-to-be-formed Soviet Union was to remain Communist right up until 1991 (see the *Events* part of the book).

CHINESE COMMUNISM

Many people describe the fall of the Soviet Union as the end of Communism, but that's very misleading. China – officially the People's Republic of China – has been governed by a Communist regime since 1949. With 20 per cent of the world's population living in China, this means that, because of that country alone, a lot of people are still living under Communism. The Chinese Communist Party was formed in 1921, in Shanghai, and one of its original members was Mao Tse-Tung. Mao was chairman of the first government council when the Communists came to power and, from 1960 until his death, was chairman of the Communist Party. An incredibly powerful and influential figure, he organized the Cultural Revolution in 1966, during which he published *Quotations of Chairman Mao* (better known as *The Little Red Book*). The idea of this 'revolution' was to achieve pure Communism by force, getting rid of those officials and party members who weren't as true to Communist ideals as it

was thought they should be – with the young betraying the old and the old the young.

THE USA AND COMMUNISM

Much of the United States' foreign policy over the last hundred years has been concerned with the suppression of Communism. The island of Cuba, lying close to the shores of the US state of Florida, is itself a Communist country, which really annoys a lot of Americans. Whether in Korea, Vietnam or Nicaragua, the US has always supported – either militarily or financially – those fighting a Communist regime or Communist rebels. The importance of the 'space race' (see the *Events* part of the book) had as much to do with trying to beat the Communists – in the form of the Soviet Union – to the moon, as the achievement in its own right. In the 1950s, the attempts to weed out Communists in the US itself resulted in the Senator Joseph McCarthy's 'witch hunts' in which hundreds of Americans were accused of being Communists and were **blacklisted**, often simply on the say-so of others. In 1954, McCarthy was finally disgraced into ending what many thought of as a 'paranoid' crusade.

THE GRIM REALITY

To many older people, the word 'Communism' will always conjure up images of drab streets, a lack of advertising hoardings, food shortages, secret police and people's attempt to escape or **defect** to the West, away from

Communist regimes. They will have memories of the Cold War – between the Communist Soviet Union and the capitalist West – where battles weren't fought with guns but with spies and propaganda. There are those who see little difference between Communist leaders and Fascist dictators, and they may have a point, but this is far removed from Karl Marx's *idea* of Communism: a fairer world for ordinary people.

PSYCHOANALYSIS

23 SEPTEMBER 1939, LONDON, ENGLAND

Sigmund Freud has died. A Jewish Austrian, he fled his homeland the year before, to escape the Nazis, and settled in England. His death makes the world news, as he was one of the greatest and most original thinkers of his generation. His creation of psychoanalysis is a completely new approach to what makes a person's personality, based on the fact that each of us has unconscious as well as conscious thoughts that make us what we are.

CONSCIOUS THOUGHT

Most of the time we're aware of what we're doing. I'm writing this and you're reading it, for example. Most of the time we know *why* we're doing something – or, at least, we think we do. I'm writing this because I'm an author and I want to share some of these exciting world-changing ideas with you, the reader. You're reading this either because you were told to, because you want to, or because you're bored and you've got nothing better to do. But you probably know – or *think* you know – why you're doing it. Your mind, and therefore *you*, is conscious of why you're doing something.

THE UNCONSCIOUS

The founder of psychoanalysis, the Austrian Sigmund Freud (1856–1939), argued that we all have a *unconscious* mind as well – that there's a part of our brain that has a big effect on why we do certain things *without our realizing why*. For example, if you had all four books from the *WOW!* series in front of you, and were equally interested in inventions, discoveries, events and ideas, what might have made you pick this one out to look at first? There could be 101 different reasons but they could include the fact that you particularly like the colour of the cover of this book. It could be that this was the same colour as a tricycle you had when you were very little. Now, here's the important part. You don't look at the book and consciously think to yourself: 'the cover of the book is the same colour as the tricycle I had when I was very little. That trike made me feel very happy, so this colour – and in a way this book – does too'. Your conscious mind may simply think 'this book looks nice', whilst *unconsciously*, it's for the reason I've just said.

IRRATIONAL FEARS

Now apply the same idea of the unconscious mind to more serious matters in a person's life. Some people grow up with what, to other people, seem very strange phobias (irrational fears). There are people who are frightened of birds, spiders, and even buttons. Most of us have at least one such phobia, but it doesn't stop us getting on with our everyday lives. But it's *not* so easy for people with a fear of open spaces, or of confined spaces, or of crossing roads or even talking to other people. If such people could be helped to overcome their fears, then they could lead normal lives. Sigmund Freud argued that, in most cases, the reason why most people have these irrational fears can probably be traced back to an event or situation in the person's past. He suggested that the unconscious mind had a reason – a starting point – for these phobias, usually rooted in early childhood.

LOOKING FOR ANSWERS

Sigmund Freud then went one stage further and said that, if a person could be made to *remember* this original cause of, for example, the phobia and be made to face it and make sense of it, then he or she could be helped to be cured of it. (As an adult, the person would have more experience and be better equipped to make sense of and understand something which simply upset or frightened him or her as a child.) This is the basis of psychoanalysis.

THE APPROACH

Psychoanalysis is often described as being an 'analytic therapeutic process', but don't panic! That's a complicated way of saying something more easily explained. 'Analytic' simply means that this is a process of analysing things: examining them very carefully, so as to understand them. 'Therapeutic' means that the process is a part of a treatment. So, as an analytic therapeutic process, psychoanalysis is a way of looking at a person's state of mind, trying to find an explanation as to why things are the way they are, interpret what it means, and then to make changes to 'cure' that person. Unlike many other treatments, however, it is the patients themselves who have to make the changes – with the help of the psychoanalyst – in order to get better.

THE IMPORTANCE OF DREAMS

Freud also believed that, under the influence of the unconscious mind, rather than a person's thoughts being abstract concepts – such as 'a fear of cheese' – they may be played out like a drama and, in these dramas-in-the-mind, certain objects may be replaced and represented by other objects, or symbols. Unlike in conscious thought, there's no obvious logic to the thoughts and images produced by the unconscious. This, Freud claimed, helped to explain what dreams were – dramas played out in the unconscious mind – and he believed that analysing dreams was a very important part of psychoanalysis.

ID, EGO AND SUPEREGO

With conscious and unconscious thought at work inside us, Freud and others were keen to try to explain exactly what 'I' means when we talk about ourselves. According to psychoanalysis, there are three constituents of the personality: the id, the ego and the superego.

- The id contains the urges and drives that originally come from our bodies and not our minds – our desire to eat when hungry, for example.
- The ego is what does the thinking, and reacts to the world around us. In an effort for the ego (and us) to function as normally as possible, the ego has a number of defence mechanisms. These include repressing (burying in the unconscious) things it can't cope with right now. (According to psychoanalysis, anxiety is an extremely important emotion because it makes the unconscious mind protect you in many different ways.)
- The superego's job is to modify or hold back any drives or impulses that the id has which might result in a person behaving antisocially – badly towards other people. It's the superego which is supposed to give us our positive image of what we could be: our ideal self.

FREUD, THE PERSON

Sigmund Freud's most famous work, *The Interpretation of Dreams* was published in 1900 and outlines all the key concepts in his approach to psychoanalysis. It was based on three years of self-analysis in which he wrote down his own dreams and then attempted to analyse them. Five years earlier, he'd published *Studies on Hysteria* with the Viennese

physician Josef Breuer, explaining their work with hysterical patients. In this they describe how patients were hypnotized and 'taken back' to events which had originally caused the **hysteria**, and made to act them out and then sort them out. You can see how this helped lead Freud to his theory of psychoanalysis. Not everyone was convinced by these extraordinary new ideas, however. Although Freud was a qualified physician and **neurologist**, there were many people in the medical profession who thought his 'psychoanalysis' was pure hocus pocus/bunkum, but belief did grow.

CARL JUNG

One of Freud's earliest and most famous pupils was Carl Jung (pronounced 'Yung'). He later took his approach to psychoanalysis off in a different direction to Freud's, creating what he called 'analytical psychology' (known by some as Jungism). He believed that there were two distinctly different parts to the unconscious mind: the personal unconscious (containing the unconscious memories of the individual) and the collective unconscious (the 'reservoir of the experience of the human race'). He also put forward the belief that there were two different types of personality: introversion and extroversion.

Introversion is when a person's interests are turned in on himself or herself. Extroversion is when they're turned out onto the world. Most people go between the two. Introverts and extroverts, however, Jung argued, were people suffering from an imbalance.

MORE SCHOOLS OF THOUGHT

Alfred Adler, also a pupil of Freud, went off in yet *another* direction. His belief was that everything anyone does is based on him or her feeling inferior to – less important than – everyone else. Babies feel inferior because they can't feed themselves, Adler argued, and they then grow up trying to be as good as everyone else around them. Fellow student Otto Rank, on the other hand, introduced the idea of neurosis. Since then, many other schools of psychoanalysis and psychiatry have grown up all over the world.

IT MAKES YOU THINK . . .

Today, there are still many people from all walks of life who believe that Sigmund Freud's ideas were, at the very worst, completely wrong or, at the very best, seriously flawed or misguided. It is undeniable, however – whether one is a believer in psychoanalysis or not – that the development of Freud's theories changed the way we think about the thought process and ourselves, and has led to a healthy debate in trying to understand what it is that makes us what we are.

ASTROLOGY

It's now or never. Hitler must make his decision. Britain has been
the thorn in his side, holding out against V2 rockets fired from the
Continent and from bombs dropped from the air. The British Royal
Airforce has defeated his own Luftwaffe and, whilst the rest of
Europe seems to fall easily into his power, this tiny, pathetic island
nation is standing up to the might of the Third Reich! It's time to
act! Should he order the invasion of Britain by sea. Surely, yes? But
wait – what do the stars predict? The planet alignments are ill-
favoured. No! The attack must wait, if it ever comes . . .

ALL IN THE STARS

Did Hitler really never invade
Britain because of astrology?
Some say that the story is
nonsense. Others say that it's
astrology that's nonsense, but
it's been with us for thousands
of years. Astrology is the idea
that the movement and position of
planets can actually have control
over people on Earth, and that events
can be predicted by the studying of them. This shouldn't
be confused with astronomy, the scientific study of stars
and planets. Today, to *most* people astrology is little more

201

than a bit of fun, looking up your general horoscope in the paper to see what the astrologer says the day has in store for you. In the past, though, astrology could decide the fate of nations.

HOROSCOPES

A personal horoscope (showing the positions of astronomical bodies at the time of a person's birth) is mapped out inside a special circle called an ecliptic, which represents the path of the Earth's orbit around the sun in a year. This is divided into twelve sections, each named after one of the signs of the zodiac listed on page 203. ('Zodiac' comes from the Ancient Greek *zoidiakos kuklos*, meaning 'circle of animals'.) An astrologer then plots the position of twelve 'heavenly bodies' (ten planets, plus the sun and the moon) within these zodiac signs. Each heavenly body is supposed to represent a specific human drive, and each sign of the zodiac a particular personality type. The zodiac sign in which the sun appears on your chart is called your sun sign. This depends on the day of the year you were born, and people born under particular sun signs, sometimes referred to as 'star signs' (the sun being a star, don't forget), are supposed to have particular characteristics. The ecliptic is further divided into twelve 'houses', with the position of the heavenly bodies within these houses giving revealing information as to a person's health, travel etc.

SIGNS OF THE ZODIAC
and 'sun sign' birth dates

Aries (the ram):

21 March–19 April

Taurus (the bull):

20 April–20 May

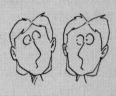

Gemini (the heavenly twins):

21 May–21 June

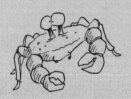

Cancer (the crab):

22 June–22 July

Leo (the lion):

23 July–22nd Aug

Virgo (the maiden):

23 Aug–22 Sept

Libra (the weighing scales):

23 Sept–23 Oct

Scorpio (the scorpion):

24 Oct–21 Nov

Sagittarius, (the archer):

22 Nov–21 Dec

Capricorn (the goat):

22 Dec–19 Jan

Aquarius (the water carrier):

20 Jan–18 Feb

Pisces (the fish):

19 Feb–20 **March**

EARLY ASTROLOGY

The idea that the study of the moon, stars and planets might give clues as to the future seems to have been thought of **independently** in different civilizations at different times. Possibly the earliest form of astrology was studied in Babylonia (now southern Iraq) 5,000 years ago in 3000BC. By 1,000 years later – that's 2000BC – the Chinese had their own form of astrology, and then it cropped up everywhere from the Indian continent to the Americas.

BUT WHY?

We can never know for sure the reason why the movement of planets was seen to be so significant by so many different peoples, but we can have an educated guess. For a start, in the days before automatic lighting inside and out, far more people would have spent time staring up at the night sky, wondering what all those stars were. And, also, people would have come to learn that the success or failure of their crops had to do with how much sunshine they got – and if the sun was responsible for growing crops, who was to say that the moon and planets didn't have other responsibilities of their own? The Babylonians knew about five planets, those which we now call Jupiter, Mars, Mercury, Saturn and Venus. Perhaps because it looked red, and people look red and flushed when they're angry – we even use the phrase 'seeing red' today – they associated Mars with anger, aggression and war.

ANOTHER 'SCIENCE'

In Ancient Greece, astronomy (the 'proper' scientific study of heavenly bodies) was in existence before astrology, and when astrology reached the Greek shores – in about 500BC – philosophers, such as Pythagoras, simply included it alongside their other sciences. This was also the case in the Middle Ages in Europe. Although the Church was quick to condemn astrology as not fitting in with Christian teaching, it was still taken very seriously right up until the early sixteenth century. It was only when people such as Copernicus and Galileo started understanding why the Earth and the heavens behaved the way they did – with the Earth orbiting the sun and not the other way around – that some of the glamour and magic rubbed off astrology and it became less and less important. (You can read about Galileo in the *Discoveries* part of the book.)

ONE OF MANY GUIDES

In Ancient Roman times, astrologers were just one of many different types of foretellers of the future. As well as astrologers there were 'haruspices', who were priests believed to have a special skill at understanding the insides of sacrificed animals. (For example, the condition of a sacrificed animal's liver was thought to tell a great deal about the Roman gods' attitude towards the government's policies!) Then there were augurs, who 'told the future' by studying cloud shapes or flocks of birds, and the ever-popular fortune tellers who could read your palm or have you throw special fortune-telling dice. But it was usually to the astrologers that the Roman emperors turned, when wanting warnings of possible assassination attempts!

NOSTRADAMUS

One of the most famous astrologers of all time was the Frenchman Michel de Notredame (1503–66), better known by the Latin version of his name: Nostradamus. He was regularly consulted by the Queen, and later **Dowager** Queen, of France, Catherine de' Medici. In 1555 he wrote a  book called *Centuries*, which contained prophecies of events that would happen during the following centuries. Fans of Nostradamus argue that he foretold many events, including the rise to power of Adolf Hitler in Germany in the 1930s and the assassination of US president John F. Kennedy in 1964. Others point out that these predictions – each foretold in four-line rhymes – are so vague and ambiguous that you could make them fit a whole series of events once they'd happened!

ASTROLOGY TODAY

Today, there are those who genuinely see astrology as an important way of guiding their own lives, and there are those who see it as a multi-million-pound industry. Top newspaper astrologists get paid top money and there are a huge number of books, magazines, CD-ROMs and websites given over to astrology. Some are very serious, some are very colourful and some are plain crazy.

BELIEVE IT OR NOT

Many people – including me, I confess – don't believe in astrology. They don't look at newspaper horoscopes, and are saddened when otherwise perfectly normal people ask them what star sign they are. To them, it's complete and utter tosh. But that's not the point. The point is that many important people throughout history *did* believe it and astrology did influence *their* decisions and, therefore, major events in world history as well as, eventually, leading to the serious study of astronomy and other sciences. And here's a thought to consider: it's the pull of the moon – a 'heavenly body' – that controls the tides of our seas and oceans on Earth . . . and our bodies are made up of about 70 per cent water, so who's to say that the moon doesn't exert some physical influence on us too? No one can claim to have a definite answer to *that* one.

MONEY

The cost of shares has been rocketing these past few months, with investors clamouring to buy more, in the hope that their value will go even higher – and then they can sell them at a profit – but now the confidence has gone. The shares are over-valued and in the past few days it's been 'Sell! Sell! Sell!' Today, panic selling is at its worst. Ten billion dollars has been wiped off the value of shares. Thousands of people have lost their investment. Many are left bankrupt, with not a cent to their names. Some will commit suicide.

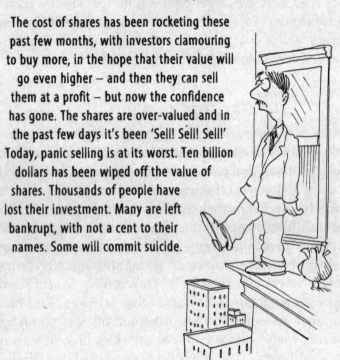

A VALUABLE IDEA

Money is an idea which grew. It's an idea which means that something which, in itself, isn't necessarily worth much – a twenty pound note isn't made of twenty pounds'

worth of paper, ink and metal strip, if you think about it –
now has a totally different value. It's a value not just
accepted by the giver and the receiver, but by the whole
society using that currency of coins and notes. A fifty pence
piece only has value because we've accepted it has that
value.

A LICENCE TO PRINT?

Something that people often ask is, when a country is short
of money – say it's at war and needs to buy weapons or
food – why doesn't its government simply print more
money and spend that? Good question. The answer is that
if a government prints more money, left, right and centre,
it devalues that currency – in other words, if a twenty
pound note is just another printed paper product like a
comic or a newspaper, then why should anyone see it as
having any more value than a comic or newspaper? People
lose confidence in it. That is why countries often used to tie
in how much money they had in circulation – in all the
banks, tills, purses, wallets, piggy banks, pockets, etc., etc. –
with how much gold the government had in their vaults. In
other words, for every penny in circulation in a country,
there was a penny's worth of government gold. This was
called the 'gold standard'. But times change. Today, with
international trading of currencies and stocks and shares,
it's the strength of a country's **economy**, and a
government's control over it (by regulating **interest** rates
and spending), that determines the strength or weakness of
one country's currency – the value of their money –
compared to another.

THEIR WEIGHT IN GOLD

Of course, there was a time when coins themselves were made of gold and silver, so the amount of money the coin represented was also the genuine value of the coin itself. This is why some old rogues used to 'clip' coins. That is, they trimmed the edges off coins to collect the gold and silver, whilst still being left with a coin with the same face value. ('Face value' is the value we give a coin – what's written on it: 'twenty pence' or 'one pound' for example – rather than its real worth.) To avoid clipping, many coins were given milled edges – little lines all the way around – so it was possible to see if a coin had been clipped. Today, some coins still have milled edges, to make forging harder.

BARTER, BARTER, BARTER

Before anyone came up with the idea of money, people would barter for goods and services. If you were a fruit grower and you wanted a pair of shoes, you would end up paying for your shoes with fruit, but only if that's what the shoemaker wanted. You might end up paying for the left shoe with fruit and the right shoe by agreeing to help him mend his leaky

roof. There was a lot of give and take on both sides and just because an exchange of goods was agreed one time didn't mean that it would necessarily be agreed again. When fruit was scarce it would be worth more – it would get you more goods in exchange – than when fruit was in plentiful supply.

ALONG COME COINS

In some societies, rice, dog's teeth, or even figs came to represent a certain value and were used to pay for services, rather than people always having to barter from scratch – so they were a currency of sorts. 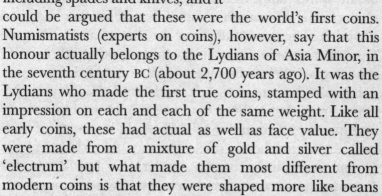 (In case you were wondering: the rice was in China, the dog's teeth in New Guinea and the figs in Ancient Egypt.) In about 2000BC – 4,000 years ago – it was the Chinese who came up with small bronze tokens in the shape of items used for bartering, including spades and knives, and it could be argued that these were the world's first coins. Numismatists (experts on coins), however, say that this honour actually belongs to the Lydians of Asia Minor, in the seventh century BC (about 2,700 years ago). It was the Lydians who made the first true coins, stamped with an impression on each and each of the same weight. Like all early coins, these had actual as well as face value. They were made from a mixture of gold and silver called 'electrum' but what made them most different from modern coins is that they were shaped more like beans than discs. The first true gold and silver coins were also made and issued in Lydia in the sixth century BC.

GREAT IDEA

Everyone knows a good idea when they see one, so coins soon caught on and were a big hit in Ancient Greece and Rome. Because the Romans ended up with an enormous empire, ruling much of the (then) known world, their currency spread to numerous countries.

Coins are very useful to archaeologists to help them date sites – a coin under a mosaic floor, for example, can be an important clue as to the earliest time that floor can have been laid.

HEADS OR TAILS

Most Roman coins included the head of the ruler or emperor on one side, a practice still common in many parts of the world today. In Britain, coins have long had a head of the ruling **monarch** on one side and another image on the other. The correct term for the side of a coin with the head on it is the 'obverse' side, whilst the other side is called the 'reverse'. When flipping a coin, though, they're more commonly known as 'heads' and 'tails'. 'Tails' probably comes from the fact that the head is the top of your body and the extreme opposite of that would be the tip of your tail – if you had one! During the rule of the Commonwealth in Britain, under the Lord Protector Cromwell in the seventeenth century, however, coins didn't have heads on them. (Neither did King Charles I – he'd had his chopped off now that Cromwell's lot were in power.) So which was 'heads' and which was 'tails' on a Commonwealth coin would be very difficult for us non-experts to guess!

A LASTING IMPRESSION

It was very important that only monarchs, emperors or governments issued coins, so that control could be kept on their value and people accepted their worth. Right up until 1500, coins in the Western world would have been hand-struck: the metal impression of heads and tails stamped by hand. It was the Italians who produced the first uniformly shaped and stamped coins. (Before then, coins were never terribly round, and the stamping was often off-centre and not too well done!) Now the Italians created a system of punching out perfectly round discs which were then stamped in special screw-down presses. All British coins were now made under strict control by the Royal Mint.

PAPER MONEY

The idea for paper money, or banknotes (what Americans call 'bills'), was probably invented by the very brainy Chinese. They were certainly using them in AD800 – that's about 1,200 years ago. According to tradition, they came about to prevent theft. When members of the Imperial Court were regularly bringing bags of money to the emperor, their horses were weighed down with all the coins so were easy targets for bandits lying in wait. They couldn't gallop away from an ambush. Paper money solved that. It was as light as – as paper, and soon gained the nickname 'flying money'. Not only could people carrying paper money easily gallop away at high speed at the first sign of trouble, but it was also difficult for bandits to tell who was carrying money and who wasn't!

TYPES OF MONEY

There are, in fact, three main types of money. I don't mean different currencies. There are plenty of them, from individual countries' currencies – pounds, dollars, lira, roubles – to a shared common currencies, such as the Euro, but I'm talking about types of money in terms of how it's valued. We've discussed them already, but here's how they're divided up and what they're called.

- The first type is when the face value of a coin is the same as its actual value. (So the face value of a gold coin, say, is literally worth its weight in gold.) This is called 'commodity money', because the coin itself is a commodity. It has value.

- The second type of money is called 'credit money'. That's what banknotes are. If you look at a British banknote, you'll find that it has 'I promise to pay the

214

bearer on demand the sum of . . .' on it. In theory, the idea is that, if you were to go to the Bank of England in London and give them a note, they'd have to change it into coins for you. But please don't try it or, if you do, please don't mention my name. I said *in theory*. In practice, that may be how the system works, but there are easier ways of getting change. It's simply that, for example, one million pounds' worth of £50 notes are far cheaper and easier to transport than one million pounds in pound coins or twenty pence pieces, so credit notes – banknotes representing that amount of coinage – are issued.

- The third main type of money has the strangest name. This is 'fiat money', and it has nothing to do with cars. Fiat money is simply money that has the face value it has because the government that issued it says so. So there. Most coins are fiat money. A penny isn't commodity money because it isn't actually worth a penny in itself, and it isn't credit money because even the Bank of England – in theory or practice – can't change it into anything smaller for you. It's worth a penny because the government says so. And that's that.

A MONEYLESS CURRENCY

Today the idea of money is as important as it's always been. We still expect to pay for things and to be paid. The big difference is that banks, building societies, shops and businesses are doing their best to encourage us not to use actual money. We can pay for things by cheque or credit card or debit card. More and more people's salaries and benefits are paid directly into their accounts – which is really the transferring of figures onto one record from another, not actually someone popping around with bags of cash. This means that we can buy things over the phone or via the internet – we don't have to see the buyer or seller face-to-face. The original idea of money completely changed the way we live and do business. Now we're probably about to enter a whole new phase in the way it actually changes hands. In the not too distant future there may be no actual money – no coins or notes – at all.

WORLD RELIGIONS

MARCH 2000, JERUSALEM, THE DIVIDED CITY

Looking old, and frail with illness, Pope John Paul II, leader of the Roman Catholic Church, is in this ancient city, sacred to Jews and Christians alike. It is here, in front of an audience of Jews and Muslims, that he makes a historic apology for the death and destruction caused to Muslims and Jews by Christians during the bloody Crusades – the 200-year religious wars of the Holy Land, fought on this very soil.

POWERFUL BELIEFS

The ideas which have probably had more influence than any others in the world's history are the ideas set out in the teachings of the world's various religions. That's why you'll find that this is the biggest chapter in all four books of the *WOW!* series. On a basic level, religion is a belief in a supernatural power (or powers) that created or rules over the universe, including people's destiny – in other words, a general belief in a god or gods. More specifically, it's an institutionalized system of expressing that belief – different organized religions (as institutions), such as Hinduism,

Judaism and Christianity, have different beliefs and different ritual ways of observing such beliefs.

PERSONAL AND SHARED

The actual word 'religion' comes from the Latin word '*religio*'. Latin was the language of the Ancient Romans (see the *Events* part of the book) who 'stole' most of their gods and goddesses from the beliefs of the Ancient Greeks, simply changing their names. The Roman king of the gods, Jupiter, for example, was the Greek king of the gods, Zeus!

'*Religio*' means the observing of ritual duties and also having a deep, inner belief, which neatly sums up the requirements of most major religions: to believe and follow a code of practice (a way of behaving) is not enough. You must express your belief by following the particular rituals of your particular faith, whether it be praying at certain times throughout the day, going through certain rights at certain ages – such as the Jewish *bar mitzvah* – or simply attending religious services.

MYTHS AND LEGENDS

What some people might see as a country's myths and legends –'traditional tales' – others might see as a part of their religious beliefs. Myths are said to be traditional stories that are based on events that didn't really happen, often containing super-humans, and that were told to help explain local customs or natural phenomena (such as why it rains, or what lightning is). Legends are slightly different in that they might be based on people who really lived, or events that really happened, which have been changed and built up into something bigger and more dramatic over time. But you have to be careful. What you think of as 'a good story' may, to someone of a certain faith, be seen as an important part in the history or teaching of their religion. They may be sacred stories or even part of their scriptures.

COMMON STORIES

Most countries have creation myths (explaining how the world came into being) and these are included in the sacred writings of many religions. This is hardly surprising. Most religions have a god as the creator of the Earth, so they need to explain exactly how that god did it. Another common theme is a terrible flood sent by a god to punish humans. The story of Noah and the Ark, filled with animals, is familiar to Jews and Christians. Ancient Greeks would have been familiar with the story of the son of the god Prometheus building a boat and surviving with his wife. Hindus are familiar with the story of Matsya the fish – actually the first **incarnation** of the god Vishnu –

warning the first human, Manu, to build a boat and fill it with 'the seed of all things'. There are similar ancient flood stories from Australia, Babylonia, China and South America, to name a few. These are a part of the sacred histories of the different faiths.

KEY EVENTS

Each of the world's main religions has a sacred history based around the key event (the most important moment) in that particular faith. In Judaism – the Jewish faith – the part most central to its teaching is the Jews' flight from slavery in Egypt (the Exodus) and Moses receiving the Ten Commandments from God. Although Christians also believe in these events, which are contained in the 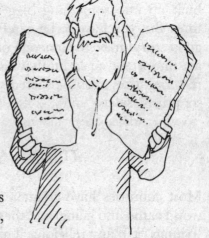 Old Testament of their Bible, the key event in their sacred history is God's coming to Earth in the form of Jesus Christ, his teachings, his crucifixion and resurrection (coming back to life). For Muslims (followers of Islam), the most important moment was when Allah (God) gave divine revelations to the prophet Mohammed, which were written down and put together to form the *Koran*. Buddhists see Buddha's moment of enlightenment as the central part of their sacred history and teachings.

A PLACE IN THE WORLD

There are some people who have no religious beliefs. They don't believe that there are any gods or deities, or that there is any life after death – whether it be as a soul in heaven or as a part of **reincarnation** (coming back as another person or animal) – a common belief in many religions. A common argument of 'non-believers' is that the various religions have grown up to feed a certain human need. In other words, if the gods aren't true, humans would have made them up anyway! Early humans will, for example, have worshipped the sun because it brought them heat and light and helped the crops grow – and they wanted to keep on the right side of it, so that it stayed friendly and came back every morning. By creating gods, they suggest, humans gained a sense of safety and belonging and, over the centuries, specific ideas and rituals have grown up around these beliefs.

WITHOUT SENDING A SIGN

Being religious is often referred to as 'having faith' and religions are sometimes called 'faiths'. This has come about because the word 'faith' means having the confidence and belief in an idea or person without necessarily having proof. In other words, religious people don't actually have to have met their god or gods face-to-face in order to believe in their existence.

TYPES OF RELIGION

Over the years, experts have tried to divide faiths into different categories. Some suggest that the earliest beliefs were probably in spirits – people thinking that most, if not all, objects from trees to water to rocks had spirits inside them. ('If I have thoughts and feelings, then why can't a tree?') This type of belief has been labelled *animism*. This then developed into a belief that there were a variety of gods controlling their lives – the sun god, the moon god, the thunder god and so on – which is called *polytheism* (*poly* means 'many'). Later, these experts reasoned, this was refined into the idea of one single god, which is called monotheism (*mono* means 'single'). But, as is true with experts in just about every subject, not all of them agree with this! Some argue that religion probably began as worshipping nature, developed into worshipping their dead ancestors and then into trying to overcome the fear of death by believing in reincarnation or the afterlife. Either approach is based on the theory that religion developed out of people trying to make sense of the world around them. If you understand something, then it becomes less frightening.

'CHURCH' AND STATE

In the past, religion was central to official life in most countries (and still is in many countries today). In most cases it was impossible to divide official religion and the state. Religion affected everything from architecture, education, painting and writing, to the clothes people wore . . . even the calendar. All the dates in this book are either BC, 'Before Christ', or AD, '*Anno Domini*", meaning 'Year of Our Lord' – the birth of Jesus being the starting point for the calendar now used by much of the world. (The Islamic calendar begins in what the Western world generally calls AD622. The Jewish calendar begins way, way back in what Christians call 3760BC.)

FROM THE CRADLE TO THE GRAVE

Even in Britain, where only a very small percentage of people regularly attend church, the trappings of religion – the rituals – are often used to mark important moments in people's lives. Couples who never go to church otherwise often want to get *married* in a church, or have their children christened (**baptized** with holy water). Again, the same can be said about death. Most British people who aren't practising Christians (but are not, of course, believers in another faith) choose to have Christian funeral services and burials – which is as much a part of the nation's culture as it is to do with any actual heartfelt beliefs.

RITES OF PASSAGE

To believers, however, these rites of passage – rituals marking significant points in their religious and personal lives – are an extremely important part of expressing their faith, and different religions have different ceremonies at different times. In addition to birth, marriage and death ceremonies, for example, entry into 'adulthood' is marked by ceremonies called *bar mitzvahs* and *bat mitzvahs* for thirteen-year-olds of the Jewish faith. Christians take their First Holy Communion or are confirmed. Many other faiths have their own rituals to mark such occasions.

HIGH DAYS AND HOLY DAYS

Most religions require followers to spend a certain amount of time celebrating and thinking about their faith. For **devout** Muslims, this means praying five times a day. For Christians, this may simply mean attending a service in a church once a week. Then there are dates in the various religious calendars that are of special significance and which require special rituals: Christmas and Easter are important times for Christians, Yom Kippur and Passover are important to Jews, and Ramadan is important for Muslims – with a whole month of **fasting** during daylight hours.

RELIGIOUS WARS

Because the teachings of many faiths are concerned with people getting along peacefully together, many people of different faiths live happily side by side. There are, however, still religion-based conflicts in the world today and, in the past, there were regular religious wars. This is one reason why the idea of religion, or religious ideas, have had such a huge impact on the world we live in today. Over the centuries, millions of people have died for their religious beliefs: Christians and Jews in the Roman arena, Muslims at the hands of Christians during the Crusades, Christians at the hands of fellow Christians during the

Spanish Inquisition, and Jews at the hands of the Nazis during the Holocaust in the Second World War. The list is very long and very bloody.

THE ARENA

A popular spectator sport back in Ancient Rome was a day at the amphitheatre watching 'the games'. An amphitheatre was a huge, round, open-air building with an arena in the centre where the actual games took place. There was a whole variety of games, but they all had one thing in common: they were violent and often very bloody. There were gladiator fights. There were fights between wild animals – and there was a real crowd-pleaser which involved unarmed 'criminals' being thrown to the lions (or other, equally vicious) wild animals. These 'criminals' were often Christians or Jews because they regularly refused to give up their own God to worship Roman gods instead. Eventually, Rome ended up with its own Christian emperor, and this activity was stopped! (See the *Events* part of the book.)

THE CRUSADES

The Crusades were the wars fought between West European Christians and Muslim from 1096 to 1291. The Christians wanted to recover the Holy Lands – what is now Israel and Israeli-occupied territory – from the Seljuk Turkish Muslims. The First Crusade aimed to recapture the city of Jerusalem, which was sacred to Christians. They succeeded in 1099, killing many Muslim (and Jewish) people living there, and ruling very harshly. Hence the modern-day Pope's apology. The Muslim leader Saladin managed to recapture Jerusalem in 1187, and the aim of the Third Crusade by the Christians was to get it back *again*. Led by King Richard the Lionheart of England and King Philip of France, they failed. There were eight Crusades in all, and they were probably as much to do with Europe flexing its military muscle to try to gain territory as to do with true Christian beliefs.

INQUISITIONS

In the thirteenth century, the 'official' Christian religion was the Roman Catholic Church, with the Pope at its head as 'God's representative on Earth'. The Church had extraordinary power and influence over the countries of Western Europe, in some instances owning as much land in a country as its monarch. Kings and queens may have ruled their own nations, but most went out of their way to stay in the Church's good books. Anyone disagreeing with the Church's statements or rulings on matters were called heretics, and what they said in disagreement was called heresy. In 1231, Pope Gregory XI (the 'XI' just means he was the eleventh pope with that name) ordered his Inquisitors to interrogate those suspected of heresy and to persecute heretics. It generally only took two alleged witnesses for a suspect to be found guilty, and there were many accusations. It was the Spanish Inquisition, which began in 1478, that resulted in the greater horrors and miscarriages of justice. Set up to weed out Jewish and Muslims who'd been forced to become Christians because of cultural pressures, it later turned into the persecution of Protestants (any Christians who'd broken away from the teachings of the Roman Catholic Church). Many thousands of so-called heretics were executed. Spanish monk and grand inquisitor Tomás de Torquemada alone ordered about 2,000 people to be burnt at the stake, and the torturing of many more.

THE HOLOCAUST

The Holocaust, when spelled with a capital 'H' (and also known as the Shoah), was the mass murder of Jewish people living in continental Europe during the Second World War (1939–45). It was a part of the Nazi dictator Adolf Hitler's plan to wipe out the Jewish race. Jewish people were rounded up and kept in ghettos before being piled into cattle trucks and taken to death camps in Poland, the most infamous of which was Auschwitz. It is estimated that approximately six million Jews died. The word 'holocaust' comes from the Latin '*holocaustum*' which means 'whole burnt offering'.

A WORLD OF RELIGIONS

There are, of course, a vast number of different religions and beliefs across the globe. Native North Americans, those people living in the South American rainforests, the most isolated tribespeople in Africa – to name just a few – have beliefs as important to them as Islam is to a Muslim or Christianity to a Christian. It's what you individually believe that is important. There are, however, a number of religions whose followers make up the majority of religious people in the world. In alphabetical order, they are: Buddhism, Christianity, Hinduism, Islam (the Muslim faith), Judaism (the Jewish faith) and Sikhism, and I thought it'd be a jolly sensible idea to end this chapter with a quick outline of each. So here you have it, the *WOW!* whirlwind guide to world religions . . .

BUDDHISM

Buddhism grew up in the sixth and seventh centuries BC in eastern North India, where Hinduism was the main religion. It's based on the teaching of Siddhartha Gautama, who became the Buddha, or 'Enlightened One'. Buddhism rejects the **Vedic** scriptures and is founded on the search for release from the endless cycle of reincarnation humans are subjected to. It believes that a person can ultimately escape being born again and again by achieving

Enlightenment. There are two main branches of Buddhism, Theravada and Mahayana, and it is practised in a great many countries, having anything up to 300 million followers.

CHRISTIANITY

Christianity is the most widely spread religion in the world, with around 1.7 billion followers – that's 1.7 thousand million Christians. Christianity is based around the life and teachings of Jesus Christ. According to Christians, Jesus was the son of the one God, who appeared in human form, and who died on the cross to give people the chance to be forgiven their sins if they followed his teachings. He is said to have risen from the dead and ascended to Heaven. Christians believe in an afterlife. The Christian scriptures, the Bible, is divided into the Old Testament (containing events before Christ's birth, which form a part of the Jewish faith) and the New Testament (starting with his birth).

HINDUISM

The main religion in India, Hinduism, was founded in 1500BC and has an estimated 700 million followers. Tribes of people, called Aryans, first settled in India in 2550BC. Over time, they settled the whole subcontinent and became known as the Hindus, which means 'of the Indus' (after the Indus valley). The Aryans' cycle of stories and teachings, passed down the centuries by word of mouth, were finally recorded in four separate collections. These became the basis for the Vedic religion. Between *c*.900 and *c*.500BC this, in turn, developed into a new religion including new Hindu gods and goddesses. (Vedic gods were still there, but playing more minor roles.) Central to the beliefs of Hinduism is reincarnation and the most important Hindu sacred texts are the *Puranas*.

ISLAM

Based on the teachings of the Prophet Mohammed, 'Islam', according to its sacred book the *Koran*, means 'to surrender to God's will'. Followers of Islam, called Muslims, believe in one God who has four main functions: creation, **sustenance**, guidance and judgement. In

return, it is the duty of human beings to give their lives to the service of God and to try to lead as pure a life and to create as pure a society as possible. On the Day of Judgement the good will go to Heaven and the failures to Hell. God, however, is forgiving and will look upon the deserving with kindness. There are over one billion (one thousand million) Muslims in the world today.

JUDAISM

Judaism – the Jewish faith – began in Israel and the surrounding lands, and the modern state of Israel offers citizenship to all Jews. There are between 12 million and 13 million Jews worldwide, and they believe in one God who continues to govern the universe. According to Judaism, God revealed his instructions to the Jews and these revelations are recorded in the sacred writings of the *Torah*, his commandments. A covenant – agreement – was made between

God and the Jews, his chosen people. The *Torah* forms part of their sacred book, the *Tanach* (sometimes called the Jewish bible and containing the same material as the Christian Old Testament), the other two sections being the *Pentateuch Nebiim* ('the prophetic literature') and the *Ketubim* ('the other writings'). A second book, called the *Talmud*, contains discussions and commentaries on the first, as well as laying down Jewish religious law. Jews are waiting for the coming of a Messiah whose arrival can be hastened by the study of the scriptures.

SIKHISM

Sikhism, the most recent of all the religions outlined in this chapter, was founded by Guru Nanak (1469–1539). Born a Hindu, he travelled with a Muslim on a pilgrimage of enlightenment, settling in the Punjabi region of India in 1520. He soon earned a reputation as a wise teacher and many came to learn from him. He taught the Unity of God and the Brotherhood of Man. His followers became known as Sikhs, which means 'learners'. After his death, there were a series of gurus, the final – Guru Gobind Singh – dying in 1708. Since then, the religion has had no spiritual leader. All guidance comes from reading their holy book the *Adi Granth*, itself called a guru and renamed the *Guru Granth Sahib*. Sikhism has over 20 million followers.

DARWINISM

12 FEBRUARY 1809, SHREWSBURY, SHROPSHIRE, ENGLAND

Almost six years have passed since the death of Josiah Wedgewood, one of the most famous British potters whose name and fine pottery will live on for many generations. Sadly, he is not alive to witness the birth of his daughter's fifth child, today. The baby – a boy – Charles Robert, will not only one day grow up to become even more famous than him, but his ideas will actually change the way that most of us see the living world around us – because this tiny baby grandson is Charles Darwin.

OUT OF THE ORDINARY

Darwinism gets its name from the British scientist Charles Darwin (1809–82). Today, most scientists and ordinary people – with the noticeable exception of Creationists, who take the story of **Genesis** to be the absolute truth – take the theories put forward in Darwin's books *On the Origin of the Species by Means of Natural Selection* and *Descent of Man* to be fact. His is the generally accepted view of how animals and humans evolved, and those who think otherwise are the ones who are often seen as the 'odd ones out'. However, that certainly wasn't the case when he first published his ideas.

MEET THE ANCESTORS

Before we go any further, it's important to dispel a few common **misconceptions** about Darwinism. Many people believe that Charles Darwin wrote a book called *The Origin of the Species*, that the 'species' referred to were humans, and that in it he stated the belief that human beings are descended from apes. The truth be told, *The Origin of the Species* is a shortening of the full title of the 1859 book *On the Origin of the Species by Means of Natural Selection* (the '*On*' was dropped when the third edition was published). The 'species' referred to are *all* species of plant and animals, not just humans, and he never wrote *anywhere* that he believed that humans are descended from apes. What he did say was that humans and apes probably had

a common ancestor. This is a big difference because, if we were descended from apes, what's stopping existing apes, such as those in London Zoo, evolving – developing over generations – into humans? This is clearly ridiculous. If, however, both apes and humans are descended from a common ancestor which died out millions of years ago – and there are far more similarities between humans and monkeys than there are differences, as modern DNA testing has shown – then there's no danger of that happening!

NATURAL SELECTION

The most important part of Darwinism, however, appears in the words at the end of the title of his book: *Natural Selection*. It was Charles Darwin's belief that the animals that are on the Earth today are the animals who have adapted best to survival. Take an imaginary example: a species of creatures – let's call them snuffles – survive by eating berries growing on a particular type of bush. They are small creatures so can only reach and eat the berries growing on the branches near the bottom of the bush. The more snuffles there are, the more berries get eaten off the lower branches and, because there aren't enough berries to go around on those bottom branches, some snuffles die. Like people, snuffles come in different shapes and sizes, so some snuffles have longer legs than others. Because longer legs mean that they can reach higher up the bush, they can get to eat more berries long after the lower branches have been stripped bare. So the long-legged snuffles survive and breed, eventually creating more long-legged snuffles, until *all* snuffles look that way – and those which were originally seen as 'normal' snuffles die out. Nature has seen to the survival of the fittest – not necessarily fittest as in healthiest but as in best adapted to suit the world around them – but it's important to remember that such changes occurred over very long periods of time.

AN IMPERFECT WORLD

The reason why this idea was so unpopular with Christians at the time – and Britain saw itself as a very Christian nation – is obvious. The Bible states that God created Adam and Eve and the animals as they are now. Darwinism states that they evolved, with the less well-adapted members of a species (and sometimes even whole species) dying out along the way. To accept Darwin's views would not only be to accept that the Bible was wrong, but also to accept that God made imperfect creatures, which couldn't adapt as well as others.

THE FOSSIL PROBLEM

The problem with backing up this widely accepted Christian view was fossils. These showed the remains of incredible creatures that weren't around any more. What were they then? These were explained by the catastrophists' theory – the idea that the Earth had been subjected to dramatic, violent changes, following natural catastrophes, the most recent of which had been the flood for which, according to the Bible, Noah built his ark. Each set of animals would have been wiped out in these disasters, and the animals on the Earth today must obviously be descended from those saved by Noah. Plain and simple.

THE AGE OF THE EARTH

Then there was the commonly held belief in Britain in the late eighteenth and early nineteenth centuries that the Earth could only be about 4,000 years old. This figure was, again, reached from information contained in the Bible, by linking people from generation to generation all the way back to Adam and Eve and the creation story. In 1785, however, a Scottish geologist called James Hutton argued that, by looking at the geological processes going on around him – the speed at which rivers wore away riverbeds or rain eroded rocks – it would have taken the world millions, not thousands, of years to end up in the condition it had then reached – and, slowly but surely, the scientific world began to listen. But rocks and soil were one thing, animals and people were quite another.

THE VOYAGE OF *THE BEAGLE*

Charles Darwin was a naturalist onboard a ship called *The Beagle* which, from 1831 to 1836, was on a voyage to survey the **southern hemisphere**, making accurate maps and records of the flora (plants) and fauna (animals) to be found in these faraway places. He started out the journey aged just twenty-two and, although he was unpaid, this was an incredible opportunity for a brilliant young mind. It was when he reached the Galapagos Islands that he made a most interesting discovery . . .

EACH TO THEIR OWN

Here was a group of islands with similar tortoises and birds on each island. But they were only similar. They were *not* the same. There were significant differences between the tortoises on each island, and it was the same with the mocking birds and finches too. They were different varieties. Now, if God had placed them there, surely they'd all be the same? Then Darwin noticed that the habitat for these creatures – the environment the animals survived in on each island – differed slightly on each island too. An idea was already forming in Darwin's mind: the tortoises and birds on each island had to adapt to fit in best with the environment of their particular island. On returning to England in 1836, he spent many years and filled many notebooks trying to make sense of the information he'd gathered. (It may seem obvious to us now, but that's because he did all the work for us!)

THE NEWS BREAKS

Darwin first shared his theories with the world when he read out a scientific paper in 1858. This was the same year that another brilliant naturalist Alfred Russel Wallace announced a similar theory, which he'd come up with quite independently of Darwin. It was the publication of Darwin's *On the Origin of the Species by Means of Natural Selection*, a year later, that really caused the sensation. All copies were sold on the very first day of publication and it quickly went through six further editions.

NO PROOF!

Darwin's ideas weren't only attacked by the Church but also by many fellow scientists. They argued that he couldn't *prove* them, which was true enough. People couldn't simply sit around and wait to see if animals evolved around them – evolution was a slow process! Then, they argued, how could animals with particularly useful characteristics – for example, the snuffles with the longer legs, in my made-up example on page 235 – so conveniently pass these characteristics onto their offspring? That couldn't be explained either. Not in those days, maybe, but with today's understanding of genetics (which you can read about in the *Discoveries* part of the book), we know that Darwin was right. Such characteristics can be passed on through **genes**.

THE LAST STRAW

What angered the Christian Church most of all, though, was Darwin's theory of 'common ancestry' and the way that he grouped human beings together with other animals. Surely the creation of human beings, at least, must have been special, and separate from that of all other creatures? Again, today we have the advantage of modern science to support Darwinism. We now know that the first true humans, *homo sapiens sapiens* – which is what we are – first walked on this Earth about 100,000 (not 4,000) years ago and that we shared the planet with a group of 'almost humans' – *Homo sapiens neanderthalensis* who died out about 30,000 years ago. They probably weren't as well suited to the environment as the bigger-brained *homo sapiens sapiens*.

THE DESCENT OF MAN

On the Origin of the Species by Means of Natural Selection has been described as 'the book that shook the world' because, in the end, it altered so many people's way of thinking about the world around them. Then, in 1871, Darwin produced his second best-known work: *The Descent of Man*. In this instance 'descent' doesn't mean the 'decline' or 'fall' of humans – Man was short for humankind, both men and women – but 'descent' as in 'descendants and ancestors', in other words: the **lineage** of the human race.

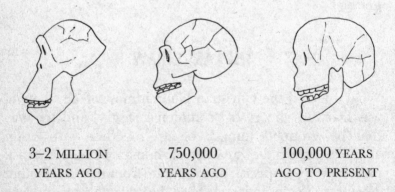

| 3–2 MILLION YEARS AGO | 750,000 YEARS AGO | 100,000 YEARS AGO TO PRESENT |

240

THE LEGACY

Today, Darwinism is taken for granted by so many that it's difficult to imagine that it's actually a group of ideas put together and argued by one man. Later in his life, Charles Darwin himself became more accepted by society in general. Today there are many scientists who are happily Christian (though not Creationists) *and* believers in Darwinism too. Charles Darwin is buried in Westminster Abbey, which was not only a great honour but also a place of Christian burial.

VOTES FOR WOMEN

4 JUNE 1913, EPSOM DOWNS RACECOURSE, ENGLAND

As the king's horse thunders around the bend in the racecourse a woman ducks under the railings and steps right into its path. What on earth's going on? What's she doing? Trying to attract attention? Make some kind of protest – or is she on a suicide mission? The crowd looks on in horror as the woman is trampled underfoot, toppling horse and jockey. She is – she was – Emily Davidson, a suffragette, fighting for the idea of votes for women. Whatever her original plan, she has just given her life for that cause. A riot will break out and over 6,000 will attend her funeral.

FAIR'S FAIR

The idea that a person can't vote in any kind of government election or referendum simply because she's a woman may seem incredible to you. That's probably because we now live in a society where everyone over eighteen who's registered – and isn't 'of unsound mind' or a prisoner serving a sentence – has that right, but it was a hard-fought one. Countries which have been held up as shining examples of **democracy**, such as Ancient Greece and Rome, were only democratic compared to other countries, because even there the men certainly didn't allow the women to elect any representatives.

KEEP WOMEN SPECIAL

That's not to say that all women thought that they should be given that right. When the idea of 'votes for women' was at its height at the end of the nineteenth and beginning of the twentieth century, there were those women who argued that it was far better for women to influence men rather than actually getting involved in the mechanics of elections. They saw women as having a unique, special and different contribution to make to society, and voting would destroy this. They were known as the 'antis' which was short for the 'anti-suffragists'. The suffragists, on the other hand, were people who believed in equal voting rights for women. The name comes from the word 'suffrage' which – far from being about pain and suffering – actually means 'the right to vote'.

ALL WALKS OF LIFE

There's a general misconception that the suffragists in Britain were all nice 'middle-class' ladies from comfortable backgrounds. However, by the 1870s, more and more 'working-class' women were members of trade unions and taking an interest in politics and rights. Many of them were also supporters of the suffragist movement. There's also another misconception that the only people championing 'votes for women' in Britain were the suffragettes, who shouldn't be confused with the suffragists. Suffragists believed in fighting for the cause by peaceful means. Suffragettes had a more **militant** approach. They were prepared to break the law. In fact, they *wanted* to get arrested so as to get in the newspapers and further the cause. Especially as, once in prison, they would often go on hunger strike to gain yet more publicity.

THE PANKHURSTS

Probably the most famous suffragette was Emmeline Pankhurst. She started out as a suffragist but, frustrated at how peaceful means didn't seem to be getting them anywhere, decided to become a suffragette and take direct action. Such action included women smashing shop windows and street lamps, burning down empty buildings and sports pavilions, slashing paintings in art galleries, pouring acid over golf courses, hassling and heckling politicians, holding marches and public meetings, and generally keeping the issue of votes for women in the public eye. Pankhurst herself was arrested a number of times between 1908 and 1913. When the First World War (1914–18) broke out, many suffragists and suffragettes put the issue of votes for women aside to concentrate on war work.

EARLY BEGINNINGS

But how did the women's suffrage campaign come to be? One milestone was the publication of *A Vindication of the Rights of Woman* in 1792, by the British writer Mary Wollstonecraft. In it, amongst other things, Wollstonecraft argued for the equality of men and women in everything from education to opportunities. A remarkable person, she spent a number of years in Paris during the French Revolution before finally settling in England. (Her daughter, also called Mary, married the poet Shelley and wrote an even more famous book: *Frankenstein* in 1818.)

Mary Wollstonecraft's *Rights of Woman* became a talking point, and a 'bible' for many early feminists.

ON THE AGENDA

During the 1830s and 1840s, suffragism really began to gather momentum. The Chartists, who were interested in all aspects of human rights – their name coming from a 'people's charter' submitted to Parliament in 1837 – were supporters of votes for women. It's important to remember that in Britain in those days not all adult men had the vote either. There were a number of requirements a man needed before having that right, and many poor and working-class men were excluded, so women's suffrage could be added to fighting for these men's causes. Suffragists also had the support of men such as John Stuart Mill (an economist and philosopher)

who, in 1865, was one of the co-founders of the first women's suffrage association. The monarch at the time was Queen Victoria but – despite her own authority and responsibilities as a woman – she was totally against the idea of women getting the vote.

UNITY AND DISSENT

It was in 1897 that the various different women's suffrage groups joined together to form the National Union of Women's Suffrage Societies. It was six years later, in 1903, that Emmeline Pankhurst broke away to form the Women's Social Political Union and its members became the suffragettes. It was almost ten years after that that Emily Davidson stood in front of the king's horse at Epsom Downs and was killed. Then came the war . . .

THE WAR IS ENDED

In 1918, the year the First World War ended, and partly due to women taking over men's jobs during that war, the

British government gave voting rights to certain women. These were 'women householders, wives of householders and women university graduates over 30'. That still excluded a lot of women, but it was a start and an incredible victory for all those people who had fought for their rights, then put aside their differences to help their country fight for a different cause. In 1928, British women were given the same voting rights as men. The battle had been won.

MEANWHILE, IN AMERICA . . .

With women excluded from voting the world over, the fight for the right was by no means limited to Britain, and many countries have their own heroes and heroines of the cause. In the US, many women wished to become actively involved in the movement to abolish slavery (see the

Events part of the book) but found that they were made unwelcome by some male campaigners. Many women then set up their own all-women abolitionist societies, but also campaigned to be heard in the more general assemblies. In 1848 the first women's rights convention met in Seneca Falls, New York. There were between 100 and 300 people there, depending on whose reports you choose to believe, but we do know that it was a mixture of both men and women. Public reaction was generally very negative and newspapers tried to ridicule suffragists as being members of a 'shrieking sisterhood'. Many suffragists were physically attacked at public meetings, which were regularly stormed by thugs. Then came the American Civil War.

AFTER THE WAR

The greatest split between the abolitionists and the suffragists came after the war, in which the American union was saved from splitting up and the slave-owning southern confederacy was defeated. Abolitionists feared that women demanding votes would make it harder for them to gain votes for freed black slaves – in other words, the women's issue was 'getting in the way' of what they saw as the main issue.

SAME GOAL, DIFFERENT APPROACHES

In 1868, there was a split within the suffragist movement itself, with the setting up of two different associations. The National Woman Suffrage Association was set up to campaign for a federal law, which would cover the whole of the US, granting voting rights to women everywhere in the country at the same time. The American Woman Suffrage Association, set up six months later, however, aimed to get voting rights for women state by state. They argued that if they could at least get votes for women in some states, it would help in the campaign to get votes in others and so on, until women everywhere could vote. This second approach had some early successes. A year later, Wyoming became the first state to give women the vote.

A CHANGE TO THE CONSTITUTION

Other states followed suit, with Colombia giving women the vote in 1893, Utah and Idaho in 1896, Washington in 1910 and California in 1911, followed by nine others up until 1918. Then in 1919, after the First World War, women in *all* states were granted the vote under the 19th Amendment to the US Constitution. The woman's suffrage amendment had been put before Congress to vote on every year since 1878, thanks to the hard work of Elizabeth Cady Stanton. As well as being the leader of the *National* Woman Suffrage Association, Elizabeth Cady Stanton, along with Susan B. Anthony, is probably one of the most famous name in the American fight for women's rights. Susan B. Anthony, who fought for the cause for 50 years, was the first woman to have her image appear on an American coin. Thanks to the efforts of these and other suffragists, suffragettes and their supporters – both men and women – women now have a voice in democracies the world over. Switzerland was the last European country to give women the vote, but women in several Arab countries still do not have voting rights today. The struggle continues.

PASSIVE RESISTANCE

30 JANUARY 1948, ACROSS INDIA

The prime minister of India, Jawaharlal Nehru, is addressing the Indian people in a radio broadcast, his voice full of emotion. 'Friends and comrades,' he begins, 'the light has gone out of our lives and there is darkness everywhere . . .' He goes on to tell the stunned and grieving audience of listeners that Mahatma Gandhi, known as 'the Father of the Nation', has been assassinated. But

Nehru has a warning. No one must seek revenge for what has happened through anger, because 'nothing would displease his soul so much as to see that we have indulged in . . . any violence.' Gandhi had helped win them their independence, only six months ago, through totally peaceful means.

OUT OF THE ORDINARY

In a world with a history filled with terrible and bloody wars, passive resistance is the unusual idea that oppression can be confronted, and eventually even beaten, by peaceful means. It is based on the principle of what Christians call 'turning the other cheek' – if you're hit on the cheek, don't hit back, but turn the other cheek and offer that one as a target too. The followers of Martin

Luther King Jr. used passive resistance to fight racism in the US (which you can read about in the next chapter). When white policemen set their dogs and then high-pressure hoses on a march made up of mainly black men, women and children, the marchers didn't fight back. If they had, it'd just have been another running street battle. As it was, the world saw pictures of ruthless white authority figures attacking innocent black people, and the impact was far, far greater.

NOT A SHOT IN ANGER

Passive resistance can work in many different ways. During the Second World War, Jewish people in countries **occupied** by the Germans were required to wear a yellow star, to be easily identified as Jewish. Not to wear a star could lead to serious trouble. In Denmark, Jewish people followed the instructions but – as a passive act of defiance – a great many non-Jewish people wore the yellow star too.

Now the Germans couldn't tell who was Jewish at a glance. When the time came for Danish Jews to be rounded up and deported to the death camps, they'd all disappeared. The other Danes had taken all 6,000 of them in small boats across the sea to the safety of Sweden. Here was a great victory without a single act of violence.

THE SEEDS OF PEACEFUL RESISTANCE

One of the first people to use the term 'civil disobedience' – a form of passive resistance involving non-cooperation with the authorities (in other words, not doing what the authorities want, but not getting violent about it) – was American Henry Thoreau (1817–62). In 1846, a part of everyone's poll tax (the tax all registered voters had to pay) went towards funding US soldiers in the Mexican War (1846–48). Because Thoreau thought that the whole war was wrong, he didn't want a single cent of his money to go towards funding it, so he refused to pay his poll tax, making it clear why. As a result, he ended up in jail. He laid out his reasons in more detail in a famous essay called *Resistance to Civil Government* in 1849, outlining how passive resistance such as his could be effective under other circumstances too. The world-famous novelist Leon Tolstoy (1828–1910) is also credited with having influenced the passive resistance movement with his writings on the love for all humans and non-violent resistance to 'the forces of evil' as defined in the Bible.

MEET MAHATMA

The greatest **exponent** of passive resistance was the Indian leader Gandhi (1869–1948) who used non-cooperation and non-violent resistance to British occupation of his country. Mohandas Gandhi, often referred to as Mahatma Gandhi – 'mahatma' means 'great soul' – described himself as a 'soldier of peace'. It's brave enough to take up a weapon and fight for your country. It's even braver to fight for your country without a weapon – especially when the enemy were the well-armed British rulers of India. Gandhi had actually been educated in Britain, and got a law degree at University College, London. Back in India, a firm with business interests in South Africa sent Gandhi there as a representative, and it was there that he developed his ideas on resisting injustice.

GANDHI IN SOUTH AFRICA

Being a 'non-white' person, he found himself being treated like a second-class citizen. (You can read about South Africa, racism and **apartheid** and its eventual downfall in the *Events* part of the book.) Gandhi was horrified by the way that Indians were treated in South Africa and committed his life to improving their plight. After being badly beaten by white South Africans in 1896, Gandhi began suggesting passive resistance and non-cooperation towards the South African authorities, calling his approach 'satyagraha' which, roughly translated, means 'defence of truth by truth'. Gandhi ended up spending over 20 years in South Africa, only leaving once many of the changes he'd so peacefully fought for – such as the South Africans finally accepting Indian marriages as legal – had come into being.

BRITISH FEARS IN INDIA

Back in his home country of India once more, in 1915, Gandhi now turned his 'satyagraha' on the British **colonial** rulers. He wanted India to rule itself. The British government was worried and, in 1919, the British parliament passed the Rowlatt Acts which gave the colonial rulers extra power to suppress any such 'revolutionary activities', violent or not. In that same year, a demonstration against the acts resulted in a terrible massacre of about 400  peaceful protesters in Amritsar, when soldiers in the British army opened fire on them. A whole series of campaigns of non-cooperation followed between 1920 and 1944, involving millions of Indians – and I don't just mean 'a lot', I really do mean *millions*. Gandhi himself was jailed a number of times. Slowly but surely, he gained attention from and then influence over the British authorities. They realized that his movement of passive resistance wasn't about to go away. Though Britain had experience of crushing armed rebellions, peaceful ones were harder to deal with.

THE STRUGGLE STRENGTHENS

'Satyagraha' didn't just mean unarmed demonstrators sitting in the street blocking traffic, and not raising an arm against their attackers if hit, spat at or even dragged away. It also meant that Indians resigned from the civil service and all public appointments. Indians wouldn't attend court if summoned, because they didn't recognize its authority. They didn't send their children to government schools. Indians also **boycotted** British goods, and people in the villages began to make more and more of their own. Knowing that many Indians would suffer many hardships when standing up to authority, Gandhi lived a very simple life himself. Not all pro-Independence Indians believed in Gandhi's peaceful approach, however, and a number of violent armed attacks on the colonial British rulers greatly distressed him. For a while, he withdrew from the cause. Finally, India gained independence from Britain in 1947, but only at the expense of it being divided into two independent countries: India (which was mainly Hindu) and Pakistan (which was mainly Muslim). This partition led to riots and it was only when Gandhi threatened to fast – go on hunger strike – until they stopped that peace was restored. Gandhi wanted friendship between religions. He always freely admitted that his beliefs had been influenced not only by his own faith, Hinduism, and by the writings of Tolstoy and Thoreau, but also by Christianity. What mattered to him was that people lived peaceful lives together as people. Tragically, in January 1948, Mohandas Gandhi was assassinated by a Hindu extremist.

PASSIVE RESISTANCE TODAY

Passive resistance is still an approach used by many pressure groups and protesters today. In Britain, many **eco-warrior** groups protesting about road-building or housing developments destroying woodland or countryside put themselves between the environment and the bulldozers – chaining themselves to blocks of concrete or living up trees and down tunnels to slow the whole process of clearing the land. Another example is of countries boycotting other countries' goods. During white apartheid rule in South Africa, many countries boycotted South African goods. They couldn't directly attack South Africa but, by peaceful means, they could damage the country's economy, trade, power and status in the world. Passive resistance can be very effective in causing world change.

AMERICAN CIVIL RIGHTS

Rosa Parks is sitting in her seat on the bus. Although both white and black people can travel on the same bus together, the rules are a clear: if a white person wants a seat and you're black, you get right up and give it to him. And that's exactly what Ms Parks is being asked to do – being told to do – day in, day out. But not today. On this particular December morning, Rosa Parks isn't about to give up her seat to anyone. It's going to get her arrested. It's going to lose her her job, but it's also going to be seen by many as the starting point of the modern American civil rights movement – fighting for blacks and whites to be treated equally.

SEGREGATION

The idea that all people should be treated equally regardless of the colour of their skin seems an obvious one. Anything else is outrageous, but it's an idea that has had to be fought for in the US through the courts, in government and on the streets. Slavery was abolished in the US in the 1860s (and you can read about this in the *Events* part of the book) but the fight for black people to be treated the same way as whites – to have the same civil rights – dates back further than that. In the past, the US was a segregated country: black people and white people lived apart, went to separate schools and often couldn't even sit on the same bench. ('Whites Only' signs seemed to be everywhere.)

DIFFERENT STATES, DIFFERENT LAWS

It's important to remember that, in the US, as well as national laws covering the whole country, states can make their own laws, unique to their own particular state. Segregation laws, therefore, varied from state to state. The laws were often referred to as 'Jim Crow' after a terrible **stereotyped** and unflattering black character from the music hall of the 1830s. (So a person might say that Jim Crow wouldn't let him do something, rather than saying segregation didn't allow it.) The southern states are more famous for their segregation, but the northern states – which fought against slavery and for keeping the states united in the American Civil War (1861–65) – had segregation laws too.

ROBERTS v. THE CITY OF BOSTON

In 1849, a man named Benjamin Franklin Roberts took the authorities of the city of Boston, in the northern state

259

of Massachusetts, to court to try to force them to allow his daughter to go to the local elementary school, nearest to his home. The problem was that Roberts and his daughter were black and the local school was for white children only. He was represented by a black lawyer named Robert Morris and by a white man named Charles Sumner. Franklin Roberts lost his case and his daughter didn't get to go to the school he wanted for her but, just six years later, segregation in all Massachusetts state-run schools was, indeed scrapped. And Charles Sumner, who'd been elected to the US Senate in 1851, went on to write the Civil Rights Act of 1875 – but that's jumping ahead.

'NON-CITIZENS'

In 1857, the Supreme Court of the United States declared that a black person couldn't be a US citizen! Before the American Civil War, black people weren't even allowed to be members of the army or navy, either. When the war started, however, many black men joined the **Union** army, in 'all black' units, such as the 4th US Colored Infantry. Despite poorer equipment and, often, less pay than their fellow white soldiers, black soldiers played an important part in the civil war, 23 of them being awarded America's highest award for bravery, the 'Medal of Honor'.

NEW RIGHTS, OLD PREJUDICES

With the war over, the northern states victorious, and the US still united, three important amendments were made to the United States Constitution. The 13th, 14th and 15th Amendments were made in 1865, 1868 and 1870 and ended slavery, made black people US citizens, with equal protection under the law, and prohibited racial discrimination in voting – black or white, you could vote (if you were a man). Most northern states scrapped segregation altogether. Sumner's Civil Rights Act made it illegal for blacks and whites to be segregated in places such as theatres and restaurants – but the unfairness and discrimination across the whole US was far from over. The problem with these national laws was trying to enforce them – to make sure they were followed – in states where white people didn't like them.

PLAYING WITH WORDS

A popular argument with those people wanting to keep black and white people separate involved the word 'equal'. Surely it was perfectly legal to have 'whites only' carriages on the railroad – as Americans call the railway – as long as there were an equal number of 'blacks only' carriages? What could be more equal than that? And if a white person could get into trouble with the law for treating a person badly simply because the person he was treating badly was black – and who was to say he might not have treated that same person badly even if he was white? – surely the law wasn't being very equal? Wasn't it favouring blacks over whites? Of course, this false argument completely overlooked that it was always the white people who had the better railway carriages, much more power and were doing the discriminating – but the US Supreme Court regularly agreed with this kind of argument and came down in favour of the segregators!

DESTROYING OF RIGHTS

Some states used even sneakier methods to try to stop black people voting, typical of which was Mississippi. Once black people had become US citizens and been given voting rights, just under 200,000 of them registered and voted – so the state introduced new rules and regulations for voters in the 1890, to try to stop them. First, anyone who wanted to vote had to pay a regular poll tax, which was far too expensive for most black people, who hadn't long been freed from slavery and were in the lowest paid jobs. Secondly, no one could vote unless they'd passed a reading and writing test. Again, this was deliberately designed to exclude black people because most of those lucky enough to have received an education (and that wasn't all of them by any means) wouldn't have received the same *quality* of education as most white people. The same was happening right across the southern states. Nowhere in the south could a black person marry a white person and, in some states, a black minister wasn't even allowed to perform the marriage ceremony of two white people.

ORGANIZED MAYHEM

Sadly, things got worse, not better. A society of white terrorists called the Ku Klux Klan – not the *Klu* Klux Klan as people often say – had been formed in the 1860s, which used dreadful violence and threats to keep segregation alive. Members wore white robes and pointed white hoods to cover their heads and hide their identity. Smaller local groups, called Klaverns, grew up and, over the years, many black people were murdered by white people, a common method being 'lynching', when the victim was hanged from a tree. (Over 2,000 were killed that way in fifteen years alone.) Many Klaverns got so out of hand that the Klan disowned them. Then the original Klan itself disbanded in 1871. The modern Klan, which still exists today, was founded in 1915.

THE NAACP

Those fighting for racial equality, meanwhile, were doing their own organizing. Following a meeting at Niagara Falls, Canada, where blacks and whites discussed ways of fighting for rights, the National Association for the Advancement of Colored People (NAACP) was formed in 1909. It was made up of a mixture of both white and black activists, and they began challenging segregation laws in courts across the land. They successfully overturned a number of laws, opening institutions like law schools as well as sections of the community to blacks as well as whites.

THE SECOND WORLD WAR

During the 1930s, vast numbers of black people left the more hostile southern states to settle in the more welcoming northern ones. Here, they encountered less racism, and better education and job opportunities. Not only that, in the south in the past, most black Americans had lived in the countryside. Now more and more of them were living and working in towns and cities, in closer proximity to each other, and nearer white people. Because black people could vote in the northern states, and in large numbers, more and more pro-civil rights and anti-segregation politicians were getting elected. Then there was the war itself: membership of the NAACP increased by 1000 per cent, newspapers published by black people for black people campaigned for victory against the fascists abroad and against the racists at home, and black and white soldiers fought alongside each other in huge numbers. Things would never be quite the same again.

MODERN CIVIL RIGHTS MOVEMENT

Then, on that December day in 1955, Rosa Parks was arrested in Montgomery for failing to give up her seat on the bus. She was an active member of the NAACP, and her branch organized a boycott of the bus service. Almost all the black people in Montgomery stopped using the buses and suddenly the bus company found itself short of about

50,000 potential customers! The boycott lasted a year and, in November 1956, a federal law was passed stopping segregation in any form on buses. All passengers should be treated equally.

MARTIN LUTHER KING JR.

The man who organized the boycott was a black Baptist minister by the name of Martin Luther King Jr. (The 'Jr.' stood for 'Junior' because his father's name was Martin Luther King too.) As well as being a committed Christian and an excellent organizer, he was also an inspiring speaker and soon became a public figure, well-known across America. He wasn't only popular with black people, but also with many white northerners. He arranged rallies, marches and demonstrations but insisted that they always be peaceful. He believed in passive resistance, the idea that violence and force can eventually be defeated by peaceful means – the idea looked at in the previous chapter of this book.

THE BASIC RIGHTS OF FREEDOM

The modern civil rights movement didn't only want to abolish all traces of segregation, it also called for freedom of speech and freedom of religious beliefs, and for these laws to be protected and enforced by the goodwill of the people in power, not simply be there on the statute book and ignored at state or county level. Based on these beliefs, Martin Luther King Jr. formed special links with Jewish and Protestant groups and his voice of protest for civil rights became louder and louder.

THE GATHERING MOMENTUM

The 1960s saw a whole variety of protests, from college sit-ins to 'freedom rides' on buses, from state to state, with many ending in violence against the protesters. In 1962, black student James Meredith won a right, through the court, to attend the all-white Mississippi University. The governor of the state, however, was against his attending and tried to stop him enrolling. Finally, President Kennedy had to supply Meredith with a bodyguard of federal marshals so that he could get into the building. Anti-black riots broke out and, along with over 300 people injured, two people actually died. When a similar incident occurred with enrolment in Alabama, in 1963, Kennedy sent in the army! That same year, a key turning point came in Birmingham, Alabama, when pictures of white police officers attacking peaceful black marchers (many of them children) with dogs and water hoses, were shown around the world.

'I HAVE A DREAM'

In August 1963, 200,000 supporters of civil rights marched through the US's capital city, Washington, DC. There,

Martin Luther King Jr. gave one of the most famous speeches in US history, which included the words: 'I have a dream that my four little children will one day live in a nation where they will not be judged by the colour of their skin but by the content of their character. I have a dream today!' President Kennedy, who proposed a new Civil Rights Act, was assassinated that November. Tragically, Martin Luther King was also assassinated, but not until 1968, and not until he had achieved much more in the fight for civil rights.

TODAY

Although one of equality's finest exponents, Martin Luther King Jr. was only one person in a series of groups and individuals who'd been fighting for change, in their own different ways, for over a hundred years. There were, for example, black leaders such as Malcolm X – himself assassinated in 1965 – who believed that equality couldn't be achieved using King's peaceful methods and should be achieved 'by any means necessary'. There are those who would argue that they are still fighting for civil rights in the US today. In April 1992, 58 people were killed and over $750 million of damage was caused in riots in Los Angeles following the **acquittal** of four white police officers. They'd been charged with the severe beating of a black man named Rodney King, and were acquitted despite the whole attack having been recorded on videotape. Even though two officers were later found guilty, many black and white people felt that this was further proof that the battle for civil rights has yet to be fully won. The US has come a long way, however, since Rosa Parks refused to give up her seat on that bus.

EVENTS
that Changed the World

For all those who made a difference

EVENTS!

Try to imagine a world where the American War of Independence never took place, so what we call the USA today is nothing more than part of the British Empire. Try to imagine a world where the Industrial Revolution never happened, so few of us live in towns or cities and most of us still work on farms to survive, or a world where slavery was never abolished and is an acceptable part of everyday life. Or a world that didn't go through the terrible loss and suffering of two World Wars . . . It's not easy, is it? That's because these are the events that have shaped our world into what it is today. In this *WOW!* book, we take a look at some of the most important prehistoric and historic events that changed the world. As for the events that will shape this new century and new millennium, who knows what they'll be? Perhaps they're unfolding right now. Perhaps you're a part of them.

PHILIP ARDAGH
2000

FIRE, FARMING AND THE WRITTEN WORD

AUGUST 1799, NEAR ROSETTA, EGYPT

Napoleon's French army has overrun Egypt, and Fort Julien is
being hastily constructed by a battalion of his engineers on
the site of old ruins. French officer Pierre Bouchard is
supervising the destruction of an old wall when he spots a
strange black stone, covered in inscriptions. Like nothing he's
seen before, he reports it to his superior officer, General
Menou. Realizing its possible importance, the General has the
find transported to Alexandria. This is the Rosetta Stone: the
key to cracking the code of ancient Egyptian hieroglyphs, one
of the oldest and most mysterious written languages in
the world.

FROM PREHISTORIC TO HISTORIC

One of the greatest events in the
advancement of humankind is,
without a doubt, when *Homo sapiens
sapiens* (modern human beings)
stepped from prehistory into
history. Prehistory (literally, 'before
history') means prehistoric times, as
in prehistoric monsters (yup,
dinosaurs) and, much, much, much
later, prehistoric 'cave' men and

women. So what exactly is history? What's the particular event separating it from prehistoric times? The answer is the development of writing, as we'll discover, but it was a long time coming. And what other prehistoric events changed our world along the way?

TERRIBLE LIZARDS

The first dinosaurs appeared in the world about 230 million years ago and after a momentous, catastrophic event – most likely a comet hitting the Earth and altering its atmosphere, blocking out the sun – they were wiped out about 65 million years ago. The world had been theirs for an amazing 168 million years. When you consider that the first upright-walking humanoid, called *Homo erectus*, only appeared about 1.8 million years ago and that the first true human beings – *Homo sapiens sapiens* – only evolved on Earth about 100,000 years ago, you realize how new we are to this planet of ours. The actual name 'dinosaur' itself is less than two hundred years old, dreamt up at a time when a real interest in their remains was starting. It was invented in 1842 by Briton Sir Richard Owen, from the Greek *deinos* meaning 'marvellous' or 'terrible' (take your pick) and *sauros* meaning 'lizard'.

MARVELLOUS

THE FIRST TRUE HUMANS

No one can say with 100 per cent certainty *exactly* when the first true humans evolved. 100,000 years can only be an approximate figure – and some experts now believe that they appeared before then – but about 100,000 years ago is a good starting point. *Homo sapiens sapiens* weren't the only human-like people around at that time, though. They shared the planet with a less brainy bunch called the Neanderthals (*Homo sapiens neanderthalensis*) but, whereas the *Homo sapiens sapiens* survived from then on, the Neanderthals died out. Although they'd been around before *Homo sapiens sapiens*, they disappeared about 30,000 years ago. Why? Because, back then, it was only the fittest, smartest and most organized who survived.

HUNTER-GATHERERS

In the beginning, *Homo sapiens sapiens* – whom I'm now going to refer to as 'people', because that's exactly what they were – were what experts call hunter-gatherers. No prizes for guessing how they got that name. They hunted animals and gathered fruit, berries and vegetables. They were always on the move, looking for more animals to kill and fruit to gather. Animals were not only a source of meat but their skins made good clothes and their bones and antlers could be used as tools and weapons too. But it was a hard, dangerous life. If you didn't die of hunger or disease a wild animal might get you first.

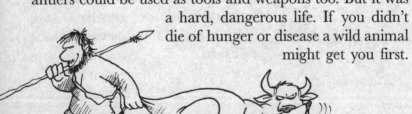

FIRE!

The discovery of fire must have been an unbelievably important event for prehistoric people. The only reason why it doesn't appear in the *Discoveries* part of the book is because we know so little about it. It's the same with spoken language. We know that over time grunts must have become words and then sentences, but much of it is supposition (which is a big word for 'guesswork' – but 'guesswork' based on some pretty educated reasoning). The early humans' first encounter with fire – and what it could do – was probably as a result of lightning. Lightning strikes a tree. The tree catches fire. People go and investigate. They see that fire is bright. They feel that fire is hot. They see that it frightens away animals and discover that those animals caught and burnt by it have tasty, soft flesh which

is much easier to tear off and chew than the raw meat they're used to. The next step is to keep feeding a fire so that they always have a source of flame for this newly discovered wonder, giving them light, heat, protection and cooking. Later, they discover a way of creating their own fire with a spark of flint.

A STUNNING IDEA

Then came an event so important yet so simple that, when you look back at it, it's incredible to think what an impact it had on absolutely everything that followed. After 89,000-ish years of people hunting and gathering and forever being on the move, people began to settle down and create farms. (That's 11,000 years ago: 100,000 – 89,000 = 11,000.) Interestingly, this was happening in different parts of the world amongst different people but at about the same time. Instead of people having to hunt animals for food, they bred animals in captivity so that they were there when they needed them. They took the biggest and best seeds and began to grow crops. People could stay put, and staying put meant that they could turn their attention to other things.

CREATING A COMMUNITY

Whereas, in the past, *everyone's* job had been to hunt or gather or both, not everyone on a farm needed to do the same job. Some people could look after the animals, others could look after the crops. Some people could make pots to hold the milk from the animals or store the seeds for crops. Others could turn their attention to keeping the gods happy, whilst some might commit themselves to designing better tools or making better clothes. Now that people were staying in one place, they needed proper homes, so a skill at building wood and mud houses developed. And people had time to decorate: make pictures, designs and patterns on objects around them. This was the beginning of real multi-skilled (lots of people with different talents doing different things) communities.

BASIC RECORD-KEEPING

Now that people were living together in these farming communities, it became necessary to start keeping basic records of who owned what. The most basic form of record-keeping was cutting a notch in a piece of wood, bone or antler for, say, each animal owned or each jar of corn stored. Once the numbers got very high, though, wouldn't it be easier to use a cross or a squiggle to take the place of a certain number of notches?

A NEW ERA FOR HUMANKIND

Then, just 5,500 years ago, these notches became more and more complicated and writing began to take shape. Then, sometime before 3000BC, the first true written language was developed in Sumer, Mesopotamia (which is now a part of Iraq) and was written on clay tablets with a pointy stick, not on paper.

GETTING BETTER ALL THE TIME

Rather than an alphabet, Sumerian writing was made up of symbols. In the beginning, these symbols were little pictures representing animals, plants and objects, including 'bird', 'sun', 'grain' and 'oxen' (all ideal for record-keeping). Over time, these pictures became simplified and stylized (looking less and less like the object they represented) until the symbols developed into cuneiform writing. 'Cuneiform' means 'wedge-shaped'. This is because the stick now used to press the writing onto the clay tablets was a special wedge shape.

EGYPTIAN HIEROGLYPHS

The Ancient Egyptians developed their writing about 100 years later and were possibly influenced by the Sumerians, though it might have developed separately. Over time, ancient Egyptian hieroglyphs became a highly complicated and sophisticated written language, covering monuments, walls, temples and scroll upon scroll of **papyrus**. So many examples of these hieroglyphs remain today that experts have been able to study them in great detail. There are over 6,000 separate glyphs (which is the name given to the symbols), and they have three different functions. Glyphs can be used as ideograms, phonograms or determinatives.

● With an ideogram, what you see is what you get. A glyph of an owl means owl!

- Phonograms represent sounds which, when put together, make up the sound of a word. This is how our alphabet works. For example, the letters 'd', 'o' and 'g' represent the meaningless sounds 'd-' '-o-' and '-g' but, when put together, mean that tongue-lolling, tail-wagging creature we know and love!
- Determinatives are the glyphs that go at the end of a word, helping the reader *determine* what the word is all about. (For example, the glyph of a seated woman at the end of a word means that the word has to do with a woman or girl.)

Ancient Egyptian had no gaps between words, didn't use **punctuation** and could be written left to right, right to left or top to bottom! And all of this was worked out and published by Frenchman Jean-François Champollion in 1824 thanks, primarily, to the Rosetta Stone. (Inscribed in hieroglyphics *and* Greek, it provided a way of translating hieroglyphics.)

THE ALPHABET

At the same time that the Egyptians were first writing in hieroglyphs, a system of writing, now called Proto-Elamite, was developed in Elam, in what is now Iran. Ancient Chinese developed about 1400BC. Each and every one of these languages was based, in some way or another, around picture symbols rather than a simple **phonic alphabet**. It was the Ancient Greeks who, in about 800BC – 2,800 years ago – developed a system of writing based solely on an alphabet. The advantage of such a system is that, in English, for example, you only need an alphabet of 26 letters to make up the 40-or-so sounds that go together to make up every single spoken word in the English language. In Chinese, however, where a phonic alphabet isn't used, you need to know about 3,000 characters to be able to read a newspaper from cover to cover.

STEPPING INTO HISTORY

And so we've reached the last big event in a chapter full of them. The dinosaurs have been wiped out, humans have appeared, they've discovered the use of fire and settled down to farm and to build communities, and now they have writing – and prehistory is at an end. Why? Because history means events that took place in a time when things could be written down and reported – a time when we no longer simply have to rely on archaeological evidence but can also study records written by human beings. In other words, in the 100,000 years that human beings have been on Earth, only events in about the last 5,500 years count as history, and that's less than 5.5 per cent of our time here!

THE RISE AND FALL OF ANCIENT ROME

15 MARCH 44BC, ROME

After being a **republic** for over five hundred years, Rome is now being ruled by the 'dictator for life', Julius Caesar. There are those who see him as a great soldier and a great leader – a unifier of the people with the people's interests at heart – and those who want to see a return to a republic as quickly as possible, even if that means killing this man who stands in its way. Julius Caesar should have listened to those warnings and bad omens, for now he is ambushed and stabbed repeatedly – twenty-seven times in all – before falling dead to the ground. But the republic will never return.

THE FOUNDING OF ROME

The first Romans got their name from the city of Rome, though they were originally from a tribe called the Latins (which is why Romans spoke Latin). The city grew up from seven separate villages on seven hills, which eventually merged into one big city. No one knows for sure when this happened, but legend has it that Rome was founded in 753BC, so it probably was round about then. The legend goes that a pair of abandoned baby boy twins, Romulus and Remus, were found by a she-wolf who brought them up and cared for them. When they were grown up, they planned to build a city on the spot where the she-wolf had found them. After a petty argument, though, Romulus killed his brother Remus so he built the city alone, became its sole ruler and called it 'Rome' after himself. The city of Rome is in the country we now call Italy, about six miles inland, on the River Tiber.

FROM FOREIGN KINGS TO A REPUBLIC

The city of Rome was originally in a region called Latium but wasn't just lived in by Latins. There were Etruscans (from the neighbouring region of Etruria) living there too. In fact, very early in its history – I'm talking well over 2,500 years ago here – the city of Rome found itself being ruled by Etruscan kings. The last one of these was said to have been kicked out in 510BC or 509BC. At that time, Rome declared itself an independent republic and nothing to do with the rest of Latium. The other cities in Latium (Alba Longa and Laurentum) didn't like this one bit, so joined forces to attack the Romans. At first, the Latium alliance had the upper hand but, by 400BC – after 100 years of fighting on and off – it was Rome that'd doubled the size of its territory and was now the most dominant power in the region.

THOSE GALLING GAULS

In 387BC, people from northern Europe, called the Gauls, invaded Rome. According to the Roman historian Livy (writing over 300 years later), most Romans fled, leaving just a few troops and the **senators**. To the utter amazement of the attacking Gauls, the Roman senators simply sat around in their garden courtyards looking as calm as calm can be. When one of the Gauls prodded a senator's beard to check he was real, the senator hit him with his stick! There was then a terrible massacre in which all the senators were killed and most of Rome was destroyed. Only the buildings on the Capitoline Hill (one of the seven) remained standing. Why? According to legend it was because geese in the temple on that hill heard the enemy coming under the darkness of night and honked in alarm. This gave those few Romans left in the city enough time to organize enough gold to bribe the Gauls to go away!

PYRRHIC VICTORIES

By 380BC, the Romans had rebuilt much of the city and added a wall around the seven hills. They also managed to regain their power in the Latium region, defeating the other cities in battle. There then followed forty years of war against the Samnites (326BC–286BC), in which the Romans not only defeated them, but also the Gauls and the Etruscans. Then, in 282BC, the Pyrrhic wars broke out. These were named after a person: King Pyrrhus of Epirus (in northern Greece). Although Pyrrhus defeated the Romans in 280BC and then again in 279BC, an enormous number of his soldiers were killed along the way. He's famous for having said, 'One more such victory and we'll be lost!' Today, the term 'Pyrrhic victory' refers to a victory won at too heavy a price. By 264BC, though, the Romans were the genuine victors and Rome was now the main power in Italy. The Latin language and Roman culture and influence spread right across the country.

THE THREE PUNIC WARS

Although the Romans were the top power in Italy, the top power in much of the western **Mediterranean** were the Carthaginians from the North African coastal city of Carthage. In 264BC, a series of wars broke out between the two peoples. The first Punic war – named after the Latin word for the Phoenicians, the founders of Carthage – lasted from 264BC to 241BC and was won by the Romans. They not only won lots of money off Carthage (a kind of payment for damages) but were also given the island of Sicily, their first territory

286

that wasn't part of Italy. A few years later, Rome seized Sardinia and Corsica too. The second Punic war (218BC–201BC) began when the Carthaginian General Hannibal famously brought his army of 35,000 troops and 37 elephants over the Alps to attack Rome! (Only one elephant made it. The other 36, along with 10,000 men, died along the way.) Despite this, Hannibal was an amazing General, winning victory after victory. In sixteen years of fighting though, he never conquered the city of Rome itself. In the end, the Romans conquered Carthaginian-ruled Spain. Now *they* were the top power in the western Mediterranean. The third Punic war (149BC–146BC) was much shorter than the others. Carthage itself was burnt to the ground by the Romans and the region became a Roman **province**! In 146BC the Romans also destroyed another city: Corinth, marking the beginning of Roman rule in Greece under a Roman **governor**. From 133BC to 31BC – that's over 100 years – the Romans took over most regions in the Mediterranean, all the way from Spain to Egypt.

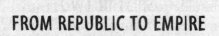

FROM REPUBLIC TO EMPIRE

From the removal of the last Etruscan king in 510BC or 509BC to Julius Caesar – possibly the most famous Roman of all – becoming dictator in 44BC, Rome was technically a republic. From 146BC to 78BC, in particular, this republic was in crisis, with various attempts to wrench the power away from a citizens-elected senate. Caesar was appointed dictator for life in the February of 44BC but he was murdered just one month later, in an attempt to restore the republic, but this wasn't to be. After years of civil war, Julius Caesar's adopted son, Octavius, was made the first Emperor of Rome in 27BC and given the new name of Augustus. Now Rome was an empire.

EMPIRE AND CIVIL WAR

The empire grew and grew and – you guessed it – grew, until it was at its height (had its most territory) during the reign of Emperor Trajan, who ruled from AD98 to AD117. The trouble was, the bigger the empire became, the harder it was to control. There was a period in Roman history known as 'the Anarchy' 118 years later. After the murder of the emperor, an army leader called Maximus Thrax (a **barbarian**) was declared emperor, but he'd not only never set foot in Rome, he could hardly speak a word of Latin either! Not surprisingly there followed a series of civil wars. The Anarchy ended with the declaration of General Diocletian as emperor in AD284.

SPLIT IN TWO

Diocletian made a number of radical changes, including making the army bigger and responsible for the administration of the empire, and the provinces smaller

and easier to administrate. His biggest change, however, was to split the empire in two. He would rule the East and a man called Maximian would rule the West. It didn't stay this way for long. Diocletian and Maximian retired in AD305. Six years later, there were still four people squabbling for the right to rule.

THE CHRISTIAN CONSTANTINE

A soldier named Constantine defeated his main rival and become an emperor in AD312. He reunited the territories, turning them back into a single empire, with him as the sole Emperor of Rome from AD324 to AD337. He moved the capital of Rome away from the city of Rome in AD330 to the newly built city of Constantinople (named after himself, but now called Istanbul, in Turkey) and declared himself a Christian on his deathbed in AD337.

AND FINALLY

Thereafter, the empire was divided, united and divided again into east and west, with the barbarians attacking and overrunning various territories. AD476 saw Romulus Augustulus, the last emperor of Rome's Empire of the

West – named after Romulus the legendary founder of Rome – deposed by a German soldier, who declared himself to be king of Italy, thus completing the fall of the Western Empire. Meanwhile, the Empire of the East became known as the Byzantine Empire, a flourishing Christian empire, with Constantinople as its capital. Its most famous ruler was Justinian (AD527–565), who managed to reconquer much of the Rome's old territories in the west too. In AD1453 – that's good old 1453, as in just over 500 years ago – however, the Muslim Turks conquered Constantinople and any remaining links with the Roman Empire, founded way, way back in 27BC were broken.

Since they ruled so much of the world for such a long time, the Romans' influence on all aspects of life is immense. They brought towns and cities to many countries which had previously only known village and country life. Their long, straight roads influenced later road-builders and even, some say, railway-builders. (The gauge, or wheel-width, of many railways is 143 cm – apparently the fixed width of Roman wagons, designed so their wheels would fit in the ruts that built up in the roads.) Later, influential architects followed the Roman design for buildings, whilst artists copied their paintings and sculptures, particularly during the **Renaissance**. Ideas of Roman law and government also survive around the world today, and then there is the Roman language, Latin, the basis for many words in many languages, including English. The stamp Ancient Rome has left on the world is almost impossible to calculate (from the Latin word *calculus*, meaning 'a pebble used as a counter'). See what I mean?

THE INDUSTRIAL REVOLUTION

JULY 1815, SOMEWHERE IN CHESHIRE, ENGLAND

The meeting is a secret. Those gathered call themselves
'Luddites' after General Ned Ludd, the man who first
organized the movement back in Nottingham in 1811. But is
Ludd his real name? Does he exist at all? That doesn't
matter. What matters is the machinery that is being
introduced everywhere – the machinery which is doing the
work that men and women used to do. It must be smashed.
Destroyed. That's what this meeting is about: making final
plans before another attack on the new machines in a
textile mill. If they're caught, they could be **transported** or,
worse still, hanged. But the Luddites are prepared to stand
and fight. It's a lost cause. By 1816, they will all have
disbanded. Industrialization is here to stay.

A DIFFERENT KIND OF REVOLUTION

Not all revolutions involve people armed with makeshift
weapons storming palaces or freeing prisoners from
jails, or even men with large moustaches firing revolvers in
the air. The word 'revolution' has other meanings. One is
'a drastic change in methods and ideas', and that's exactly
what the Industrial Revolution was: the changing of first
Britain, then western Europe and the USA into industrial
nations.

FARMING

Ever since our first farmers settled down 11,000 years ago (back on page 278), farming remained the backbone of all civilizations. People had to eat to live, so much of the land and a great deal of time and effort went into raising crops and animals for food. A rich medieval baron might have had fine castles and an army of knights wearing his **coat-of-arms** and fighting in his name, but he also needed plenty of land and serfs (labourers who couldn't leave the land they worked on) to farm it to keep him in his wealth. The Church too expected payment in the form of tithes – a percentage of the crops a person grew. To be really rich you needed to own a vast amount of land and to turn much of it over to food production. Land equalled riches. The Industrial Revolution was to change all of that.

AGRICULTURAL ADVANCES

The Industrial Revolution started at the beginning of the eighteenth century – in the early 1700s. It partly came about as a result of the Agricultural Revolution in Britain. Better farming practices and equipment was being invented, including everything from seed drills for planting, to bigger and more efficient ploughs. Farms themselves were being restructured with landlords renting land to farmers, who then paid labourers to work it. Suddenly, the same amount of land was producing much larger quantities of food. In other words, there was (what people who like to use big words would say) increased agricultural productivity. And what was the result of this? That even more people could be freed to work elsewhere.

INVENTION AFTER INVENTION

As well as people inventing machinery that could make the farmers' lives easier, people were also inventing machines that would revolutionize the manufacturing (making) of goods. In 1733, John Kay invented the **flying shuttle** which doubled the amount of weaving a weaver could do in a single day! In 1764, James Hargreaves's spinning jenny – a wheel which allowed one person to spin many different threads at once – could make a typical spinner spin sixteen times faster! Then, in 1769, Richard Arkwright developed something called the 'water frame' – which, powered by a watermill, pulled fibre from cotton and spun it into thread on a frame – completely revolutionizing the amount and quality of cotton twine and material produced. Meanwhile, the steam engine and locomotive went from strength to strength and iron production was improved and increased.

FROM COUNTRY TO TOWN

Suddenly, industries were beginning to use new and improved machinery which, with a big enough workforce to operate it, could lead to an increase in production beyond anyone's wildest dreams. This mechanization (use of machinery) led to the building of huge mills and factories, and of homes for the workers to live in. Before the Industrial Revolution, most people lived in towns and villages in the country, which are called 'rural communities'. In fact, in 1800 there was only one city in the whole world which had more than a million people living in it, and that was London. Now that people were leaving farming and the countryside to work in the factories, towns and cities – urban areas – grew and grew. By 1900, there were ten cities in Britain with populations of over a million and the world's urban population had tripled.

IMPROVED CONDITIONS?

This move to the towns would ultimately mean improved living conditions for most people, but it was a long while coming. Old farm workers' cottages in the countryside may look picturesque today but since they were unheated, unlit, leaky-roofed and without sanitation, many can't have been much fun to live in. A move to new purpose-built homes near a factory probably seemed like a dream come true to some people. Of course, there were problems of overcrowding and poor sanitation in these new urban developments, and some were little more than slums, often within the shadow of huge factory chimneys belching out black smoke . . . but things did get better eventually.

FROM LANDED GENTRY TO INDUSTRIALIST

Now a person could be rich without owning any farmland. He – and it was just about always a 'he' – could be a mill, steel foundry or factory owner. He was not a member of the landed gentry, whose land and wealth went back generations, but was an industrialist and a capitalist, making his money from the production and selling of goods. Many of this new class of person made their wealth on the backs of poorly paid workers. In the north of England, the main industry was cotton. The big new mills of the early nineteenth century meant that profits soared, but workers' wages remained the same. They had no share in this new-found wealth. Some industrialists, however, were great **philanthropists** and were keen to create excellent living conditions for their workers, encouraging education as well as good housing.

IRON ROADS OF THE REVOLUTION

The spread of the railways in the 1830s (which you can read about in the *Inventions* part of the book) not only opened up whole new markets to these new **mass-produced** clothes and other goods, but also helped the growth of the iron and steel industry. Someone had to supply all the metal to make the machines and build the tracks. Then there were steam ships to be built too. Engineering industries were cropping up everywhere. The Industrial Revolution had quickly spread through France, Belgium, Germany, and the United States by the middle of the nineteenth century, and reached Sweden and Japan by the end. Industrialization then began in Russia, Canada and beyond in the twentieth century.

THAT'S SOME REVOLUTION!

So what were the effects of the Industrial Revolution on the world? Massive. It introduced new approaches and new technology, with the careful application of both practical and scientific knowledge to the manufacturing process. The Industrial Revolution, therefore, changed the whole nature of production – what was produced, where and how – and switched from production of primary products (such as corn) to the production of manufactured goods and services. There were now more manufactured goods than ever before. This revolution not only altered countries' economies but also their societies with large clusters of enterprises now located within vast towns and cities. Most revolutions of the overthrowing-the-government variety haven't achieved such world-wide changes as that!

THE AMERICAN WAR OF INDEPENDENCE

25 DECEMBER 1776, DELAWARE RIVER, NORTH AMERICA

No Christmas celebrations here. It is night and, under the cover of darkness and a terrible storm, General George Washington, the man who will one day become the first President of the United States of America, is leading a small army of just 2,500 men across the ice-choked river and on to victories against British forces at Trenton, and then at Princeton. News of these successes will boost the morale of the **American Patriots** fighting for their independence against their English masters.

A GROWTH IN SIZE AND DIFFERENCES

The American War of Independence (1775–83) was fought between the inhabitants of the thirteen British colonies and their 'masters' who laid claim to North America: the British. There were a whole variety of different reasons as to why the colonists finally had enough of their 'mother country'. For starters, the sheer number of colonists had grown beyond all recognition. The first colony was established in 1607. By 1700, there were about 250,000 colonists. By the 1770s there were ten times as many which, if my maths is any good, means 2.5 million of them! Not only that, far fewer of them had a British background than before. While the New England colonies of Connecticut, Rhode Island, Massachusetts, and New Hampshire were still very British in numbers of colonists and their way of life, most other colonies were made up of Europeans from elsewhere. There was also the fact that about 20 per cent of the population of the North American British colonies was now black, because of slavery. That's over 565,000 people. Understandably, they had absolutely no loyalty to Britain.

RELIGION

There was also a real mish-mash of different religious beliefs. Whereas the original Pilgrim Fathers who came from England – see the *Discoveries* part of the book – were low church Protestants, the colonists had splintered into a variety of different Protestant groups over the years, and Roman Catholics and Jewish people had also settled there. What this meant for North America's British masters was that it was harder for them to please and control such a large number of people from such different backgrounds and with such different beliefs.

DIFFERENT COLONIES, DIFFERENT RULES

In the 1750s, a colonist's first loyalty was to his or her colony, not to Britain. Each colony had its own governor and law-makers. There were, by then, three types of colony: corporate, proprietary and royal.

- If you were a white, property-owning man living in a *corporate colony*, you could not only vote for who sat in the colony's assembly – all colonies had one – but also for the colony's governor and council members.
- In a *proprietary colony*, however, you weren't ruled by elected council members but by descendants of those who originally founded the colony. The governors were still chosen by the British.
- The *royal colonies*, which made up eight of the thirteen British colonies had governors appointed by the king, and – except for Massachusetts – the council members were nominated by the king-appointed governor and approved by the British Board of Trade.

There wasn't one policy making British governing body to affect all thirteen colonies, or to make the inhabitants feel a part of Britain.

THE ASSEMBLIES

Each colony, whatever its type, had its own assembly. While its British masters ruled on matters such as trade and foreign affairs, the colonists were pretty much left to their own devices when it came to local laws and taxes. The British thought that such fairness would leave the colonists contented, while what it actually did was to create an excellent **forum** for those colonists wanting to break free of Britain to have an independent North America. In the meantime, the British rather ignored the colonies, leaving the colonists to their own devices.

THE SEVEN YEARS' WAR

Then 1756 saw the outbreak of the Seven Years' War in North America – and no prizes for guessing when it ended. Yes, seven years later in 1763. It wasn't the colonists against the British but the British against the French. It wasn't so much a proper war as a number of separate skirmishes, centred mainly around the northern colonies. The British were eventually victorious and gained land in Canada and Florida, but the war had been expensive and they found themselves in debt. Who better to turn to for money than the British colonists? The British looked at North America with renewed interest, introducing new laws and taxes and reinforcing old ones. The colonists resented this heavy-handed interference.

STAMPING AUTHORITY

A whole series of British laws followed, declaring what the people of the North American colonies could and could not do. Then there was the much-loathed Quartering Act of 1765 which meant that colonists had to house, feed and supply British troops quartered (stationed) in their areas. In other words, they were expected to pay for and support what many of them considered to be an occupying foreign army! Worse was yet to come. The Stamp Act meant that colonists had to buy special revenue (tax) stamps and stick them on everything from legal documents and newspapers to playing cards!

GONE TOO FAR

Many colonists decided that enough was enough. Here they were having to pay British taxes drawn up by the British parliament without being able to vote for any MPs to represent them in that parliament. In other words, as their slogan put it, this was: 'taxation without representation'. In October 1765, delegates from nine of the British colonies met in New York for an anti-Stamp Act meeting called the Stamp Act Congress. They sent a petition to the king, George III, asking him to scrap the Act. Others colonists took more immediate drastic action, destroying stamps, forcing tax officials to resign and, in Boston, an angry mob even destroyed the home of the lieutenant governor, Thomas Hutchinson. Britain was losing its grip on the colonies.

NO TURNING BACK

Many British merchants wanted the Stamp Act repealed (scrapped) too. All this unrest was losing them trade with the colonists, and they wanted things to go back to the way they had been. Now more and more colonists were boycotting British goods. Unfortunately for everyone, rather than repealing the Act, a newly elected British government, under Lord Rockingham, confirmed that the British had the right to tax any of their subjects – which included the inhabitants of the thirteen British colonies in North America – whether they had the vote or not. So there. Yah boo sucks.

A TAX ON TEA

Despite Britain's attitude, a peaceful solution did seem possible as far as some of the colonists were concerned. American colonist Benjamin Franklin – who was such a general all-round amazing guy that he also appears in the *Discoveries* part of the book, for his work on electricity – declared, in his role as statesman, in 1769 that Britain should: 'repeal the laws . . . recall the troops, refund the money . . .' A new British government, this time under Lord North, went some way towards easing the pressure. However, the troops remained and, to remind the colonists that the British could tax what they wanted whenever they wanted, they put a tax on tea. This led people from different colonies joining forces, and more and more people expressed their pride in being American.

THE BOSTON TEA PARTY

In November 1773, with the British tax on tea in force, three British ships arrived in Boston harbour with a cargo of 342 chests of tea in their holds. If they were unloaded, the colonists would have to pay duty (tax) on each chest. So the citizens of Boston refused to unload them. The governor of the colony of Massachusetts, however, refused to allow the ships to leave *until* they'd been unloaded and the duty paid. There was a stalemate – until, on the evening of 16 December, a group of colonists crept aboard the ships and tipped all the tea out of the chests and into the water. Led by the American Patriot Samuel Adams, many of them covered their identity by disguising themselves as Native Americans!

THE RIDE OF PAUL REVERE

Things swiftly moved from bad to worse. The assembly of the colony of Massachusetts was supposed to meet in Boston but began to meet illegally in Concord. In 1775, British troops were ordered to go to Concord, to close down the assembly and arrest the ringleaders.

A group of American Patriots – including a man named Paul Revere, later made famous in a poem by Longfellow – rode through the night from Boston to Concord to warn them that the British were coming. The message got through (though, unlike the story told in the poem, Revere himself was stopped by the British) and the colonists were ready for the troops when they came. The troops retreated to Boston with over 270 casualties, whilst the Patriots lost less than a hundred people.

DECLARATION OF INDEPENDENCE

The colonists made one last attempt at peace, but the British would have none of it. They put a **naval**

blockade around the colonies so that no trade could go in or out. Englishman Thomas Paine, who settled in America, pointed out how ridiculous it was that a tiny island should continue to try to rule a huge continent! A 'Continental Congress' had been formed, made up of representatives from the various colonies on the North American continent and they chose a man named George Washington to lead the Continental Army. On 4 July 1776, they issued the Declaration of Independence, which explained the reasons for breaking away with Britain and declared that the colonies were now the free and independent United States of America.

PROS AND CONS

Mistakenly, the British believed that they could win this war with brute force. Not only did Britain have a huge army compared to the numbers the Patriots would be able to call up to fight, but there were also still those colonists in America loyal to the British cause, along with some Native Americans who'd never liked the colonists in the first place. The Americans, on the other hand, had the advantage of being familiar with the territory they were fighting on – they knew the lie of the land. Not only that, the Patriots later received funding from Britain's old enemies in America: France and Spain. But it was true to say that the American soldiers were few in number and very badly fed and clothed, and often never paid. No wonder there were often **mutinies** against the American Generals! But the longer they fought, the better organized they became and the more battles they won.

THE FOUR PHASES OF THE WAR

Looking back on the American War of Independence, war historians have divided it into four distinctly different phases: Phase One, from April 1775 to July 1776, was when the American Patriots managed to turn what started out as little more than a small rebellion into a full-scale revolution, with the British and **Loyalists** trying to keep them down. (The worst fighting between the Patriots and Loyalists was in the south where, for a while, civil war reigned. It was also during this first phase that the Patriots invaded Canada. Though failing to take Quebec, the American army became better organized during this part of their military campaign.) Phase Two began in July 1776 with a massive British invasion of New York and ended with a British defeat at Saratoga in October 1777 (seen by many as the real turning point in the war). Phase Three began at the start of the following year with British forces concentrating on seizing land in the south and leaving the Loyalists to defend it. At this stage, the Patriots used very effective guerrilla tactics against the British and, with the French, won a memorable victory against them in Yorktown, Virginia in October 1781. Phase Four, the final phase, was a time for American diplomacy.

WINNING THE PEACE

After the humiliating surrender of British troops at Yorktown, the British government was growing tired of war. They would have to raise taxes at home to support a further war effort and knew that this would be most unpopular with the voters. Although a few skirmishes continued here and there, the final two years of the war were taken up trying to sort out a peace acceptable to everyone. It was officially declared that Britain would no longer be involved in 'an offensive war in America' and the British government opened negotiations with the Americans – as I'll now call them – and their French allies. On 3 September 1783, the Treaty of Paris was signed, in which Britain kept Canada and won rights for British traders in America, and promises for the protection of Loyalists who'd fought alongside them in the war (in fact, 100,000 of them left America, taking their wealth with them). Britain now fully acknowledged the independence of the United States of America.

WORLD SUPERPOWER

It really goes without saying why the American War of Independence was such a world-changing event because, today, the USA is the most powerful country in the world. It had a long way to go to get there after 1783, from the writing of the Constitution to the swearing in of George Washington as their first president in 1789, through the American Civil War (1861–65) – with North against South, **Unionist** against **Confederate** –

the abolition of slavery and the struggles of the civil rights movement, through to the present day, but get there it did and is now the central country on the world stage.

THE RISE AND FALL OF
THE SLAVE TRADE

OCTOBER 1854, SPRINGFIELD, ILLINOIS, USA

The young man standing on the speaker's platform is wearing no collar or tie and has his shirt sleeves rolled up in a business-like fashion. He is here to speak out against an act passed by the United States government which extends slavery when, in his opinion, it should be banning it. 'When the white man governs himself, that is self-government,' he says, 'but when he governs himself, and also governs another man – that is **despotism** . . . my ancient faith teaches me that "all men are created equal", and that there can be no moral right in connection with one man's making a slave of another.' The speaker's name is Abraham Lincoln. Less than seven years later, he will become the 16th President of the United States of America.

THE MOST TERRIBLE TRADE

The European trade in African slaves – kidnapped black African people who were snatched from their homes, shipped abroad and forced to work in often terrible conditions for no pay – lasted for almost 400 years, during which time a staggering 15 million slaves were taken to the Americas – North and South – to work on plantations on land belonging to the various empires. Millions more died

308

in the vessels, nicknamed 'coffin ships', that were supposed to take them there. Slavery is one of the worst examples of human beings' inhumanity to human beings, but it wasn't until the late eighteenth century that the anti-slavery movement was born.

THE BIRTH OF SLAVERY

Slavery goes back to the earliest civilizations with slavery common in ancient Egypt, Greece and Rome. The spread of Roman power meant that slavery went with it and, right up until the eleventh century, slavery still existed in Britain. Even in the 'New World', Mayan, Inca and Aztec societies relied on slaves, as did the ancient Indians and Chinese. But it was the Portuguese who began the African slave trade in the early 1440s.

THE AFRICAN SLAVE TRADE

Portugal was short of people to work the land and saw black Africans as an ideal source of labour. To begin with, these slaves were Africans caught by other Africans who sold them to the Portuguese at a string of forts and trading posts established along the western coast of Africa. By 1460, about 800 slaves a year were being shipped to Portugal and, remember, these 'slaves' were frightened kidnapped men, women and children. North African Arab traders soon saw the money in slavery and, throughout the fifteenth century, shipped slaves seized in central Africa to markets in Arabia, what is now Iran and the Indian continent. The Spanish soon started trading in people too, but for over 100 years, the Portuguese were the main slave traders.

THE TRADE WITH SPAIN

Having colonized parts of South America in the late sixteenth century, the Spanish wanted slaves to cultivate the land. The obvious choice were the native South Americans themselves, such as the Aztecs, but, unfortunately, many of them were soon wiped out by the diseases brought by the Spanish. Because these diseases were new to South Americans, their bodies didn't have any natural resistance to them. Not only that, they were worked so hard under such hot and humid conditions that many died of exhaustion. The obvious solution was to buy African slaves off the Portuguese, already used to working hard under such conditions. Britain entered this terrible trade when it won the contract to supply African slaves to the Spanish through the British South Sea Company in 1713.

NORTH AMERICAN SLAVE TRADE

The first African slaves brought to North America came to work in Jamestown, Virginia – the first permanent, successful English colony to be set up in North America – in 1619. They were few in number and had the same legal rights as some Native American and white servants, though there was nothing they could do about having been kidnapped and taken from their homeland against their will. As the number and size of plantations grew in the southern colonies of North America, the 'need' for slaves grew too, though many slaves in the north were used for domestic chores.

TREATING HUMANS LIKE ANIMALS

Quite apart from the cruelty of the very idea of slavery itself and the dreadful overcrowding and conditions in the ships bringing them from their homelands, there were other appalling practices in the keeping of slaves. Some slaves were branded like cattle – they had their owner's brand burnt into their skin with a hot iron. Others were forced to wear slave collars, or walked in shackles to stop them running away. Owners killing slaves was not uncommon either. Despite this, slaves in North America were supposed to have some basic rights. By the time of the American War of Independence, the rights and responsibilities of the slave owner and slave were clearly laid out, even if they were often ignored.

AN END TO THE TRADE

When looking back from the twenty-first century to the eighteenth- and nineteenth-century slave trade, it's difficult to imagine why every decent person didn't think that it was a terrible thing and should be abolished. The traders themselves might have been motivated by greed, along with the big plantation owners who were getting cheap labour, but what about all ordinary men and women? Surely they were horrified by what was going on? There were certainly 'kind' slave owners who treated their slaves 'well', but what on earth were they doing keeping slaves in the first place? This is often the problem with looking back in history. It's easy to forget that people then were brought up in a totally different climate and culture to how we are today. For most white Europeans, slavery seemed a normal part of everyday life. It was fortunate, therefore, that there *were* men and women who believed it was wrong even then, and spoke out against it.

MR SHARP AND MR STRONG

Granville Sharp was born in Durham, England, in 1735. His grandfather was the Archbishop of York and his father was an archdeacon, but Sharp didn't want a career in the church. After a brief spell in the clothes trade, he became a clerk in the civil service. His whole world was turned upside down one day, though, when he was staying in his brother's house in Wapping, East London. The year was 1765, and Granville Sharp's brother was a surgeon. One day, a man was brought to the house because he'd been pistol-whipped – very badly beaten with the butt of a pistol. His name was Jonathan Strong and he was a black slave, brought over from Barbados. The man who'd beaten him was his master, David Lisle. Granville Sharp took Jonathan Strong to St Bartholomew's Hospital where he remained for four months – yes, *four months* – to recover from his serious injuries.

TAKING ACTION

Amazingly, when Jonathan Strong was discharged from hospital and fully recovered, his master Lisle paid two men to go out and recapture him! Granville Sharp was so horrified that he took Lisle to court, claiming that since Jonathan Strong was in England where there were no slaves (there were only slaves in the colonies), Strong was no longer a slave so couldn't 'belong' to anyone. Although it took the courts until 1768 to agree with him, the case gained plenty of publicity and opened up the debate of the rights and wrongs of the slave trade. Granville Sharp, meanwhile, took up the causes of men in similar positions to Jonathan Strong, such as Thomas Lewis and James Somersett.

VOICES AGAINST SLAVERY

Having long since resigned from the British civil service, because he supported the American colonists in their fight for independence, Granville Sharp decided to form *The Society for the* **Abolition** *of the Slave Trade*, with his young friend Thomas Clarkson. Born in 1760, Clarkson had become a strong believer in the abolition of slavery after winning a 1785 Cambridge University essay competition entitled 'Is it right to make men slaves against their will?'. Both he and Granville Sharp were members of the Church of England but of the twelve members on the board of their newly formed society, nine were **Quakers**. Clarkson managed to get hold of leg shackles, branding irons and slave collars to show audiences the true horrors of slavery, and wrote a pamphlet urging the end of the slave trade.

WILLIAM WILBERFORCE

The society persuaded the MP for Hull, a man called William Wilberforce, to speak on anti-slavery issues in the Houses of Parliament. Wilberforce was to become one of the greatest names in the anti-slave trade movement. In May 1789, he gave his first anti-slavery speech in parliament. In 1791, he introduced a bill to abolish the slave trade. It was defeated by 75 votes. In 1805, Wilberforce managed to get the House of Commons to pass a bill making it illegal for any British subject to transport slaves. Unfortunately, this was then stopped by the House of Lords so didn't become law. In 1806 – after a change of government – the Abolition of the Slave Trade Bill was passed by the Lords and went back to the Commons were the voting was 114 votes for the bill and only 15 against. On 25 March 1807 it became law.

A LONG WAY TO GO

The immediate effect of this new act was that any British captain found with slaves on board his vessel was fined £100 for each and every slave. £100 was a lot of money and, multiplying it by the number of slaves, could leave a captain bankrupt. This was seen as a good way of deterring them from continuing their evil trade. In truth, some British captains carried on as slavers and simply threw slaves overboard, leaving them to drown, if they thought a British naval ship was coming. But this wasn't the only reason why the work of the anti-slavery movement wasn't over. All this law did was to ban Britain taking part in the trading of slaves. It didn't make slavery itself illegal.

1807 saw Granville Sharp and Thomas Clarkson join with a man named Thomas Fowell Buxton to form *The Society for the Mitigation and* **Gradual** *Abolition of Slavery*. The reason why they thought abolition should be gradual rather than immediate was they believed that the slaves should have time to be educated and prepared for their freedom. This was also the official view of the *Anti-Slavery Society*, founded in 1823. Others believed that all slaves in British colonies should be freed immediately.

THE WOMEN SPEAK

A number of women's anti-slavery societies were formed by women such as Elizabeth Heyrick, Anne Knight, Mary Lloyd and Elizabeth Pease. 1824 saw Elizabeth Heyrick publish a pamphlet arguing just this point: that slaves should be granted their freedom there and then. It was wrong to wait. The first anti-slavery society to actually call for the immediate freeing of slaves was the Sheffield Female Society in 1827. Many women even boycotted sugar produced on slave plantations, and this captured the imagination of the British public. In 1830, the Female Society for Birmingham called for the *Anti-Slavery Society* to campaign for the immediate end to slavery at their national conference – and, if not, the Female Society would withdraw all the funding they gave them. The Female Society were brilliant fund-raisers for the anti-slavery cause, and to lose their donation would be a big blow. At the May 1830 conference, a new campaign for the immediate freeing of slaves, led by one Sarah Wedgwood, was agreed. In 1833, the Abolition of Slavery Act became law.

THE AMERICAN CIVIL WAR

Although the USA abolished the slave trade just one year after the British, in 1808, slavery itself wasn't abolished throughout the country until 1865. In fact, the country was divided – north and south – by the slavery issue, and this led to the American Civil War (1861–65). In 1861, eleven southern states broke away from the United States, declaring themselves to be the Confederate States of America. These were the states which relied on slave labour to work on their plantations and keep their economy thriving. The newly elected president of the United States, Abraham Lincoln, said that the Confederates could not leave the Union, and that it was an illegal act. War broke out. In the end, the Confederates were defeated. More than 600,000 people had died but more than 4 million slaves were freed.

NEXT?

Over time, the slave trade and then slavery itself was outlawed in country after country across the world. As South American colonies gained freedom from their Spanish and Portuguese masters, most of these newly formed independent republics granted their slaves freedom at the same time. In 1926, the League of Nations adopted the International Slavery Convention, clearly stating that no forms of slavery should be allowed to exist. In 1948, these sentiments were incorporated into the United Nations' Universal Declaration of Human Rights. Although it is impossible to say with any certainty that there are no slaves left anywhere in the world today, we can say that the world-wide trade in millions of human beings is, thankfully, no more.

THE LEGACY OF SLAVERY

Possibly the biggest effect on the world by slavery, and its final abolition, is the huge spread of black Africans and their descendants across the globe. There are, for example, over 34 million black people living in the USA today. It is unlikely that there would be nearly that number if their ancestors hadn't been seized from their homelands and forced to work on American soil. Without US slavery, there might have been no segregation laws – separating white people from black people – and no civil rights movement, led by the likes of Martin Luther King Jr, fighting for their abolition (which you can read about in the *Ideas* part of the book). Many people simply take for granted that South American and Caribbean countries have always been populated by black people, but this isn't true. It's another example of descendants of black African slaves and freed slaves building new lives away from home. The rich variety of different black cultures, but with common roots, is one of the few good things to have come from this most dreadful of trades.

THE FIRST WORLD WAR

28 JUNE 1914, SARAJEVO, BOSNIA

Archduke Francis Ferdinand is being driven through the street of Sarajevo in his open-top carriage. He is on home ground. Bosnia is a part of the mighty Austro-Hungarian Empire, and the archduke is next in line to the thrones of both Austria and Hungary. One day, the people on these streets and in these houses will be his subjects . . . unless . . . unless . . . A man steps forward as the carriage nears. His name is Gavrilo Princip. Before anyone can stop him, he raises a weapon at the archduke, steadies his hand and fires.

A WAR TO END ALL WARS?

As their names suggest, no two wars have had more impact on the world than the First and Second World Wars. The First World War (1914–18) began as a local conflict between Austria-Hungary and Serbia but became a full-blown European and, later, *world* war when Russia and the USA were dragged into the conflict. At its height, there were thirty-two different nations fighting: Germany, Austria-Hungary, Turkey and Bulgaria, known as the Central Powers, against the Allies made up of twenty-eight nations in all, including Britain, France, Russia and the

USA. Sometimes referred to as World War I or the Great War, the First World War was also known as 'The War to End All Wars'. Sadly it wasn't.

A SHOOTING AT SARAJEVO

On the surface, the cause of the outbreak of the First World War was the murder of Archduke Ferdinand in Sarajevo. His assassin was a Serb nationalist and hater of the Austro-Hungarian Empire. This made the murder a political assassination and an international incident, and wars had been fought for a lot less in the past. The actual reasons for the war, though, were much more deep-rooted than that.

TAKING SIDES

At the beginning of the twentieth century, Germany was in dispute with Britain and France over colonies in their African empires, and more and more countries began pouring more and more money into their armies and navies in preparation for a war that they knew would come, sooner or later. They also began to take sides, forming alliances 'in case of war' which were more likely to actually *cause* war! The Triple Alliance consisted of Germany, Austria-Hungary and Turkey, and the Triple Entente was made up of Britain, France and Russia. After a few false starts, involving Germany and France in dispute over Morocco, and the Balkan Wars (1912–13) in which Italy declared war on Turkey, Archduke Ferdinand was killed in June 1914 and the First World War began a month later.

DECLARATIONS OF WAR

It officially began on 28 July 1914, with Austria declaring war on Serbia, and Russia mobilizing some of its troops ready to fight Austria. The Germans then told the Russians that if they joined the war, Germany would fight them and, when Russia refused to demobilize immediately, Germany declared war on them on 1 August. Two days later, they declared war on France. To get to France, the German army would have to march through Belgium, but Belgium wouldn't give them permission. When Germany said that they were coming through anyway, Britain declared war on Germany on 4 August 1914 (because they'd signed a treaty promising to defend Belgium's **neutrality**).

THE 'BRITISH' ROYALS

Kaiser Wilhelm (nicknamed 'Kaiser Bill' by the British) was not only Emperor of Germany and King of Prussia, but was also the son of the late Queen Victoria's eldest daughter. King George V, on the other hand, who was on the throne of *England* during the First World War, was the son of the late Queen Victoria's eldest *son* – which meant that the two heads of state were not only on opposite sides in the war but were also first cousins who shared the same granny! The British monarchy's family name at the time was Saxe-Coburg-Gotha. Fearful that it might not go down too well with the German-loathing British public, it was quietly changed to Windsor in 1917.

MANY FRONTS

The First World War was fought on many different fronts (areas of conflict). On the eastern front, Russia seized Poland as early as 1914 and looked like it was going to seize Hungary too, until combined German and Austrian forces finally forced the Russians out, causing terrible casualties. On the western front, the Germans planned to swoop through Belgium and take control of France but, after the Battle of Flanders at the end of 1914, the war on the western front stopped being a war of armies-on-the-move and turned into what the First World War is most famous for: trench warfare.

TRENCH WARFARE

On the western front, enemy faced enemy in their facing lines of **trenches**, with a barbed-wire strewn muddy no man's land in between. If an enemy bullet or shell didn't kill you, disease could, and 'going over the top' (of your trench) left you wide open to enemy fire. Huge numbers of lives were lost over gains of just a few feet of land. At one stage, the ordinary British troops on the front line were described as 'lions led by donkeys'. Throughout 1915 the Allies were on the attack, at Neuve Chapelle in March, Vimyu Ridge in May and Loos in September. The Germans were on the **offensive** in May at Ypres (which British veterans pronounced 'wipers' – it's actually pronounced something like 'eepr'). It was at Ypres that poisonous gas was used for the first time. In December of 1915, the Commander-in-Chief of British Forces, Sir John French was replaced by Sir Douglas Haig. 1915 also saw British forces invading Mesopotamia and landing in Gallipoli (in Turkey), which had to be evacuated in January 1916.

BLEEDING FRANCE WHITE

1916 was the year that German 'bled France white', starting with an attack at Verdun on the western front in February and continuing ceaselessly until June, but still failing to gain any significant ground. The Allies began their offensive in the area of the Somme river, slowly pushing forward from July to November. It was here that tanks were used in warfare for the very first time, not that they were particularly effective under such muddy conditions. A French attack at Verdun, meanwhile, helped regain the little land Germany had taken.

THE USA JOIN THE FIGHT

Early in the war, German submarines blockaded Britain, attempting to sink any ships going in or out. On 7 May 1915, they sank the passenger liner the *Lusitania*, killing a number of US passengers. On 16 March 1916, the French steamer the *Sussex* was sunk in the English Channel, killing yet more US passengers, but still the USA didn't actually enter the war. On 31 May 1916, British and German naval forces engaged in fighting off Jutland. Although the British fleet suffered more losses, they gave the German fleet such a pounding that it stayed in port for the remainder of the war! Further German submarine attacks on civilian ships carrying US passengers led to the USA entering the war, on the Allies' side, on 6 April 1917. This was an important turning point for the Allies whose troops were battle-weary and demoralized.

REVOLUTION IN THE RANKS

Russia wasn't only fighting a war on the eastern front, but had its own troubles back home. In March 1917, the **Tsar** and his family were overthrown and a new, liberal government came to power in Russia. This government wanted to continue the war, however, so soon found itself overthrown too! The new revolutionary rulers were the Bolsheviks – **Communists** who immediately pressed for peace. (You can find out more about communism in the *Ideas* part of the book.) Fighting stopped in December 1917 and Russia signed a peace treaty in March 1918. They were out of the war.

MORE GAINS AND LOSSES

Near the start of 1917, the Germans retreated to the north of the Somme to a new line of pre-prepared defences called the Hindenberg Line. In April, the Allies launched an attack on Vimy Ridge and, although they successfully captured it, the loss of human life was enormous. As a result, there was mutiny in the French ranks, with many soldiers fleeing. From July to November 1917 came an Allied advance from Ypres in the direction of the French coast. This became known as the Passchendaele offensive (after a village in Flanders) and the British suffered heavy casualties – which is 'war speak' for saying that many were killed or terribly injured.

THE ITALIAN FRONT

Meanwhile, in Italy, the Italians (who were members of the Allies against Germany) were holding up well against the enemy until October 1917. This was when combined Austrian and German forces attacked at Caporetta, forcing the Italians to fall back with terrible deaths and casualties. An Allied Council was set up to try and coordinate a more unified approach and French and British soldiers were sent to the Italian front to try to help out.

AMERICANS UNDER FIRE

In March 1918, the Germans began their final push for victory on the western front – at least, that's what they hoped it'd be – and it began very successfully. In less than three months, they'd retaken all the land that the Allies had gained in 1915, but what they'd failed to do was break through the Allied line of forces. It may have retreated, but they hadn't got through it to attack from behind. And the

Allies had reinforcements, and not just any old reinforcements. They were reinforced with US troops, fresh and ready to fight (and under enemy fire for the first time in June 1918). All Allied troops were now under the command of the Chief of General Staff, Frenchman General Ferdinand Foch (pronounced Fo*sh*, if you want to say the name out loud).

THE TURNING TIDE

On 15 July, the Germans began an offensive on Rheims. The Allies responded with an attack on Marne and, by the beginning of August, the Germans had retreated to their line of defence. By the end of August, the British had broken through it. The US then went into action as a separate, independent army alongside the French. The tide had turned.

PEACE BREAKING OUT EVERYWHERE

In September 1918, the Allies attacked Bulgaria which quickly agreed to peace terms and, the following month, they forced the Austrians out of Serbia. On 3 November, the Austrians signed an armistice (a truce to give up fighting until a proper, final treaty was agreed). Turkey had agreed to an armistice on 30 October.

REVOLUTION FROM WITHIN

There had always been those Germans uneasy with what was being done in their name, and the Russian Revolution had led to more outspoken anti-war feelings in Germany. When, in October 1918, the German fleet was ordered to prepare for action, there was outright mutiny and this spread from city to city right across Germany. Germany began to discuss peace with the Allies on 6 November and on 9 November Kaiser Bill was forced to **abdicate**.

AND IN THE END . . .

The First World War was lasted four years, three months and two weeks, ending at 11 o'clock on the 11th day of the 11th month (November) 1918, with the armistice signed in the forest of Compiègne. It had been fought on land, sea and, for the first time, in the air, with Zeppelins dropping bombs and bi-planes engaging in **dog fights**. There were over 37 million casualties of soldiers alone and another 10 million or so civilian casualties, caught up in the war in one way or another. Over 8.5 million soldiers died. The Russians suffered the worst casualties, not only in sheer numbers but also as a percentage of the numbers of troops who fought. Around 1,700,000 were killed, 4,950,000 were injured and 2,500,000 missing or prisoners. That was over 76 per cent of the number of Russians called up to fight. The USA, whose intervention in the war helped lead to the Allied victory, had, on the other hand, casualties of only 8 per cent.

BAD TO WORSE

The world after the First World War was a different place. A whole generation of young men had been killed, injured or seen such horrors that life could never be quite the same. There really was a feeling that the world had 'learnt its lesson' and that there would never be warfare on such a grand scale again – that it really had been 'The War to End All Wars'. Then 1918 and 1919 saw a deadly Spanish Flu epidemic spread across the world, killing even more people than the fighting had done. Some people saw this as 'divine retribution', a punishment from God for the First World War.

HERE WE GO AGAIN

War memorials sprang up in towns and villages across Europe, and 11th November became Remembrance Day, a day when those who fought, died or were injured were remembered. Meanwhile, Germany began to rise from the ashes of defeat. The agreements reached in the peace treaties were never properly enforced, and it wasn't long before Germany began growing into a military power again, with aggressive ideas that would lead to disruption and disorder in other parts of Europe . . . and finally to the outbreak of the Second World War.

THE SECOND WORLD WAR

29 SEPTEMBER 1938, LONDON, ENGLAND

British prime minister Neville Chamberlain steps out of the aircraft and waves to the assembled crowd. There is a cheer. He walks over to a group of waiting reporters and, speaking into a microphone, raises a document above his head. 'I have here a piece of paper,' he begins, and goes on to explain that it's a copy of the Munich Pact signed by – amongst others – Adolf Hitler, and how it will mean 'peace in our time'. He is wrong. In less than a year, Britain will be at war with Germany.

ALL NATIONS TOUCHED BY WAR

The Second World War was fought from 1939 to 1945, following the rise of the **Nazis** in Austria and Germany, led by Adolf Hitler. On the one side were the Allies, led by Britain, the **USSR**, France, China and the USA, whilst on the other were the Axis powers headed by Germany, Italy and Japan. By the end of the conflict most nations in the world had been touched by the war in one way or another.

TAKING TERRITORIES BY FORCE AND FEAR

Before the war itself broke out, Germany, Italy and Japan had been throwing their weight about a bit. The Japanese conquered Manchuria (a region of north-east China) in 1931 and then invaded the rest of China in 1937. The Italians conquered Ethiopia in Africa in 1935–36. The Germans and Italians entered the Spanish Civil War (1936–39) on the side of the **Fascists**. Then in 1936–37, treaties signed between Germany, Italy and Japan created the Rome-Berlin-Tokyo Axis, which is how they, and their right-wing allies, came to be known as the Axis powers. Then, in March 1938, Germany 'annexed' Austria, making it a part of German territory. The Chancellor of Germany and leader of the Nazi Party, Adolf Hitler, was himself an Austrian. In September that same year, Germany seized Sudetenland, which was a part of what was then Czechoslovakia along Germany's western border.

APPEASING THE AGGRESSOR

Britain and France were unhappy with what was happening but, with Germany armed to the teeth again, and a reluctance to go to war again so soon, they accepted that acts such as the annexing of Austria were 'internal affairs', and that the outside world shouldn't interfere. The USA, meanwhile, had passed a law which meant that it must remain neutral and mustn't aid any sides in foreign conflicts. Britain and France tried to reason with Hitler and his allies, with a policy of 'appeasement'. (Appeasement really meant compromise: granting Germany concessions they may not really have a right to, in the hope of keeping a wider peace.) The result was the Munich Pact, signed by Germany, Italy, Britain and France in September 1938. In it, it was agreed that Czechoslovakia should give up its Sudetenland region to Germany (after all, it contained 3.5 million German-speaking people), in return for the guarantee that Germany would not take any more Czech territory.

BRITAIN DECLARES WAR

In March 1939, Germany completely ignored the pact and marched into Czechoslovakia anyway. The Italians conquered Albania the following month. Horrified, Britain and France were eager to get the USSR on their side in case trouble escalated even further. In August, however, the USSR signed a 'non-aggression' pact with Germany, each agreeing to leave the other alone! On 1 September 1939, Germany invaded Poland. Hitler was confident that Britain and France wouldn't dare interfere. Now, *he* was wrong. On 3 September, Britain and France declared war on Germany.

POLAND AND BEYOND

After the Germans' successful invasion of Poland, with the fall of its capital city, Warsaw, on 27 September, little more happened until 1940. Then, in May of that year, Germany invaded Denmark and Norway. The British and French went to help Norway but had to withdraw when France itself was invaded in June. With the British people unhappy with the failure of the Munich Pact and all that had happened since, Chamberlain's government fell and was replaced by a government made up of members of all political parties, headed by the new prime minister, Winston Churchill. Germany's invasion of Belgium in May 1940 led to one of the most famous evacuation of troops in British history, from Dunkirk, a northern French port. During the evacuation, British and French troops, who'd been fighting German advances, were saved by a flotilla of ships which travelled back and forth across the English Channel. It was made up of everything from small fishing boats and pleasure craft to military vessels, brought across by a mixture of sailors and civilians. This makeshift navy of 'little ships' saved the lives of over 337,000 men and quickly passed into folklore. Overrun by German forces, and with Italy now declaring war against the Allies, France was forced to sign an armistice with Germany, but the French resistance movement fought on, backed by the Free French movement, lead by General de Gaulle in London – French soldiers still fighting against the Axis.

BRITAIN STANDS ALONE

With the USSR having signed a non-aggression pact, the USA committed to staying neutral, and much of continental Europe overrun by Germany, Britain pretty much stood alone against the enemy from 1940–41. Then, in August 1940, began the Battle of Britain. The German airforce, the Luftwaffe, launched bombing raid after bombing raid on Britain. They started them in daylight

but, having lost almost 2,000 aeroplanes, decided that night-time raids, under the cover of darkness, might be better! Churchill said of the British Royal Air Force fighter pilots who faced them: 'Never in the field of human conflict has so much been owed by so many to so few.' Despite inflicting terrible damage and loss of life on London, Coventry, Liverpool, Hull and many other cities, Britain did not surrender, and the bomb attacks became much fewer and far between. In 1940 the Greeks fought off an invading Italian force but, along with Yugoslavia, they were defeated by German forces in 1941, despite British assistance.

ENTER THE USSR AND THE USA

In June 1941, Germany, somewhat foolishly, now felt confident enough to attack the USSR, which meant that the latter could no longer remain 'non-aggressive' but would have to come out fighting against the Axis powers. Meanwhile, USA public opinion was more and more in favour of joining the war, on the side of the British. Then, on 7 December 1941, Japan bombed the US navy base at Pearl Harbor, Hawaii, and declared war on Britain and the USA! On 11 December, Germany and Italy also declared war on the USA!

AFRICA, THE NEAR EAST AND ITALY

1940 saw war raging in Africa and the Near East, with German forces under Rommel facing British forces under General Montgomery (**aka** 'Monty'). Here, a European war was being fought on the soil of its colonies. Monty's most famous victory was at El Alamein. When General Eisenhower landed British and US troops in Morocco and Algeria, the Axis forces were forced to surrender in 1943.

Allied forces now crossed from North Africa and invaded Italy. On 25 July, the Italian Fascist leader Mussolini was overthrown, and ended up being strung from a lamp-post by fellow Italians. On 13 October, under a new government, Italy declared war on Germany. Germany tried invading but were, eventually, defeated in April 1945.

VICTORY IN THE EAST!

The Allies' victory at El Alamein and Eisenhower's landing in Morocco and Algeria, along with the Germans' failure to capture the city of Stalingrad in the USSR are considered, by brainy military experts who understand such things, as the turning points in the war. Now the USSR went out and out against the Axis forces, killing or capturing 330,000 enemy forces at Stalingrad alone. They forced them out of Russia, entered Yugoslavia, freed Poland and Austria and entered Czechoslovakia and, from there, entered Germany itself and headed for its capital city, Berlin.

D-DAY!

Plans, meanwhile, had been underway to liberate the west. After mass air raids on Germany from 1940 onwards, the invasion was launched under the control of the now supreme allied commander, General Eisenhower, on 6 June 1944. It was codenamed 'D-Day', and began with landings on the beaches of Normandy. By the end of September, the Allies had entered Belgium and the Netherlands and liberated most of France. When the USSR reached Berlin, Germany surrendered unconditionally on 7 May 1945. Adolf Hitler is believed to have committed suicide.

THE WAR AGAINST JAPAN

The fight against Japan, however, was not yet over. Early in the war, the Japanese had control of the Philippines, Malaya, Thailand, Hong Kong, Burma and Singapore. In 1943, the Allies' attack against Japan was split three ways: Lord Mountbatten in Burma (what is now Myanmar), Admiral Nimitz in the Central Pacific and General MacArthur in the South West Pacific. By May 1945, Burma was almost completely back under Allied control and the Allies were making gains elsewhere in the region when the war against Japan came to a sudden and terrifying end. To shorten the war, the USA dropped two newly invented atom bombs on two Japanese cities: Hiroshima and Nagasaki. (You can read about this in the *Discoveries* part of the book.) The Japanese formally surrendered on 2 September 1945.

THE HOLOCAUST

From the moment the Nazi Party came to power in Germany in 1933, it began to discriminate against and persecute Jewish people. They lost jobs in the civil service and other important positions and Jewish doctors were only allowed to treat Jewish patients. One night, in November 1938, hundreds of synagogues in Germany were set on fire, the windows of Jewish shops were smashed and thousands of Jews were arrested. This event became known as *Kristallnacht* – or the 'Night of Broken Glass'. Hundreds of thousands of Jewish people fled the country, yet many more remained. The more countries Germany invaded, however, the more Jews it had within its borders. They were forced to wear yellow stars and armbands to distinguish them, but much worse was yet to come. In 1941, the Germans planned to implement 'the final solution': the murder of all Jews in death camps. Most of these death camps were built in occupied Poland, and it was here that Jews were deported – many in railway cattle trucks – from German-occupied territory. The most infamous of these camps was called Auschwitz. The total number of Jewish people murdered by the Nazis is estimated to be about 6 million by the end of the war.

THESE WHO HAVE FALLEN

One of the big differences between the First and Second World Wars was that bombing raids (by aeroplanes and rockets) brought the war to civilians in those countries not even occupied by enemy forces. It also saw the introduction of a whole new type of weapon – the atom bomb. And then there were the sheer numbers of people who had died. There were 25 million members of the military and 30 million civilians, in addition to the almost 6 million people murdered in the Holocaust. These are such large figures, it's almost impossible to think of them as dead human beings. The post-war world was also left with the birth of two superpowers – the USA and the USSR – the threat of nuclear weapons, and the formation of the **United Nations**, intended to prevent many of the original types of problem that led to the Second World War.

TO THE MOON AND BACK

21 JULY 1969, THE MOON

The world watches and waits with bated breath as American astronaut Neil Armstrong is about to become the first human being to set foot on a patch of ground that is not a part of planet Earth. Grainy black-and-white pictures are beamed from the moon to Earth as Armstrong reaches the bottom of the ladder of the lunar module *Eagle* and steps onto the moon's surface. Armstrong speaks to the world via his radio microphone set inside his helmet: 'This is one small step for man,' he says. 'One giant leap for mankind.'

THE FANTASY OF SPACE

Frenchman Cyrano de Bergerac is a famous character, with a very big nose, in a play written by Edmond Rostand in 1897. What's less well-known is that he really existed. He was a seventeenth-century writer and his works included what we now call science fiction. He wrote a story about a trip to the moon in 1656. De Bergerac wasn't the first to do this – Ancient Greek writer Lucien wrote about an imaginary trip to the moon in his *True History* (which wasn't true *or* history), over 1,800 years ago – and he certainly wasn't the last, either. Two hundred or so years after De Bergerac, fellow Frenchman Jules Verne (famous for his *Around the World in 80 Days*) wrote a book called *From the Earth to the Moon* in 1865. In 1901, Englishman H. G. Wells wrote *The First Men in the Moon*. Thereafter, comic

337

book after comic book and film after film followed with science fiction adventures of men, women and children travelling to the moon and beyond.

SOME SERIOUS SUGGESTIONS

It wasn't just the writers of fiction who were interested in the possibilities of reaching the moon. In 1903, the Russian thinker Konstantin Tsiolkovsky published a book called *A Rocket into Cosmic Space*. He was one of the first people to argue in print that the only way of getting through the Earth's atmosphere and out into space was with a rocket. In 1919 an American, Robert Goddard, published a paper called *A Method of Reaching Extreme Altitudes*, proposing a project to fire a small, unmanned (peopleless) rocket to the moon. He built a number of very small rockets, some of which went faster than the speed of sound.

THE ADVANCES OF WAR

It was the hard facts of war rather than dreams of space travel that brought the development of rocket science forward in leaps and bounds. German student Wernher von Braun had always been fascinated with the idea of rockets and space flight. He and a group of friends built and launched their own small rockets in Kymmersdorf, near Berlin. In 1932, their activities aroused the interest of the German military. The good news was that von Braun soon found himself the head of an experimental rocket station . . . the bad news was that these rockets weren't to take anyone to the moon but were to be flying bombs. The result were the V2s, which regularly landed in Britain, killing and injuring hundreds of people during the Second World War.

ESCAPE!

At the end of the Second World War, with Germany defeated, von Braun gave himself up to the US army, willingly sharing the secrets of his new rocket technology. Soon the Americans had him making rockets for them, but still only as weapons. In 1955 he became an American citizen, but 1957 was an even more significant year for von Braun, because this was the year that the **Soviets** launched the world's first space satellite – and soon the space race between the USA and the USSR would begin.

MACHINES IN SPACE

The Soviet satellite *Sputnik 1* was launched by the USSR in October 1957, and orbited the Earth. *Sputnik 1*'s full name was *Iskustvennyi Sputnik Zemli* which is Russian for 'Fellow World Traveller of the Earth'. *Sputnik 2* was launched a month later and, this time, carried a dog named Laika to see how living, breathing creatures survived in space. She was fine, until her oxygen supply ran out. By January 1958, the USA had their satellite *Explorer 1* up in orbit too. The Soviets launched

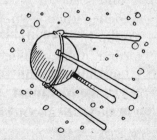

Sputnik 3 in May of that year and the space race was hotting up.

THE AMERICAN REACTION

Eager to make sure that the USA wasn't left behind in the space race, US President Dwight D. Eisenhower passed the National Aeronautics and Space Act in 1958 which, amongst other things, created NASA (the National Aeronautics and Space Administration). In 1958, both the Soviets and the Americans were unsuccessful in attempts to launch and land unmanned probes on the moon which could send back valuable information and pictures. The Soviets succeeded in September 1959 with their *Luna 2* probe. The world's first pictures of the dark side of the moon (never seen from here on Earth) were taken by a camera on board *Luna 3* launched in October of the same year. Although the USA's *Ranger 7* probe took some stunning pictures of the moon's surface in July 1964, giving the first really clear close-up pictures of the moon, the Americans were concerned that, in the space race to the moon, the Soviets had achieved all the major 'firsts' so far. In February 1966, the USSR's *Lunar 9* made the first soft landing on the moon – in other words, it didn't crash and get damaged.

A FISTFUL OF FIRSTS

NASA had launched their Lunar programme a month after Soviet **cosmonaut** Yuri Gagarin became the first person in space on 12 April 1961. The USSR seemed well ahead in the race. Especially when cosmonaut Valentina Tereshkova became the first woman in space as early as 16 June 1963. In May 1961, NASA had started the Apollo programme: an attempt to land a person on the moon and bring him – all the astronauts in their programme were men – safely back to Earth. The programme was launched by US President John F. Kennedy.

APOLLO

The Apollo missions began in 1967, and with tragedy. On 27 January 1967, three American astronauts, Virgil Grissom, Edward White II, and Roger Chaffee, died in their space craft when it was still on the ground, during a run-through of take-off procedures of Apollo 1. A fire burnt up all the oxygen in the capsule and they couldn't breathe.

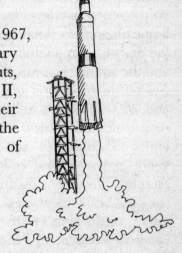

APOLLO ELEVEN – TO THE MOON!

The launch vehicles for Apollo missions – the actual rockets which blasted the men and machinery out of the Earth's atmosphere and into space were *Saturn V* rockets. These were designed by the former German V2 rocket scientist Wernher von Braun, including the rocket, launched from Cape Canaveral, which was to begin the first flight to the moon: *Apollo 11*. Once in space, the

rocket section served no
purpose and was jettisoned
from the remaining sections:
the command module
Columbia and the lunar
landing module, *Eagle*.
Whilst Neil Armstrong
and Edwin 'Buzz' Aldrin

took the *Eagle* to the moon's surface, astronaut Michael
Collins piloted the *Columbia*. If anything went wrong down
on the moon, Collins's instructions would have been to fly
home alone. The lunar module landed in a flat area called
the Sea of Tranquillity – though there was no water in it –
and the landing site was called Tranquillity Base. The *Eagle*
was on the moon for just 21 hours
and 36 minutes, of which
Armstrong and Aldrin spent 2
hours 31 minutes out and
about exploring and collecting
samples. The eight-day mission
was a complete success, the
Eagle re-docking with the
Columbia command module,
before being jettisoned and all
three astronauts returning to
Earth in a tiny capsule which
landed in the Pacific Ocean.

OTHER TRIUMPHS

After Apollo 11, probably the most famous Apollo mission
was Apollo 13, launched in April 1970. Although disaster

struck and it never reached the moon, all three astronauts managed to return to Earth safely, thanks not only to their skills but also to the skills and instructions of those back at NASA Mission Control in Houston, Texas. Mission Control first became aware of the difficulties when astronaut James Lovell announced: 'Houston. We have a problem.' The problem was that an explosion had caused the command module to lose oxygen and electrical power, and the astronauts had to move into the lunar module. Thanks to some ingenious makeshift adjustments and repairs, they made it home. These dramatic and exciting events have since been retold in the film *Apollo 13*, released in 1995, with Tom Hanks in the role of Commander Lovell.

SO FEW

So far, only twelve people have walked on the moon. The first were Neil Armstrong and 'Buzz' Aldrin on the Apollo 11 mission in June 1969, and the last were Harrison Schmitt and Gene Cernan on the Apollo 17 mission in December 1972. All were American astronauts. Once the Americans had landed there, the Soviets turned their attention to other achievements in space. Since then, there have been space shuttle flights, long stays onboard space stations and unmanned probes to the planet Mars and beyond, but none of these events have quite the excitement of watching live television pictures of a human being setting foot on the moon for the very first time – or the image of the Earth itself as seen from the moon: small and vulnerable, just hanging there in space.

THE FALL OF
THE BERLIN WALL

9 NOVEMBER 1989, THE BERLIN WALL, EAST GERMANY

Standing on top of the Berlin Wall, looking down into West Berlin, the small group of people can't quite believe it's really happening. They can't believe they're really here. A few days ago, anyone would have been shot dead by East German guards just trying to reach this point – many have died in the attempt in the past – yet here they are, on top of the wall – on top of the WORLD! Someone starts smashing at the wall, chipping away at the concrete. Yes! That's it! The wall must come down. East and West must unite. The crowds grow bigger by the minute. There is crying. There is laughter. There are cheers. The wall must come down . . .

AFTER THE WAR

At the end of the Second World War in 1945, Germany was a defeated country and its capital city Berlin was surrounded by Soviet-occupied territory. The city itself, however, was divided into four sectors: British, US, French and Soviet, with representatives from each sector on a governing board. The problem was that although the Soviets (often referred to as the Russians because Russia was the biggest country in the USSR) were on the winning side, and lost more troops than any other country in the war, they weren't trusted by their allies and the Soviets didn't trust them in return. The Soviets were communists, whilst the British, US and French were **capitalists**. This marked the beginning of the Cold War – not a war of battles and guns but of mistrust, spying and trying to get the upper hand.

THE BERLIN AIRLIFT

In 1948, the Soviets withdrew from the governing board of Berlin, and set up their own totally separate municipal government for their part of the city. They argued that there was no longer any reason for the British, US and French to remain in Berlin and, being surrounded by Soviet territory, the city should become totally part of the Soviet zone. They blockaded all the routes to West Berlin by road, railway and water, depriving West Berliners of food and supplies – but their plans were crushed by the Berlin airlift. The British and US flew supplies into West Berlin for eleven whole months, until the Soviets ended the blockade.

WARNING
BEYOND THIS
POINT IS THE
RUSSIAN ZONE

TWO REPUBLICS ARE BORN

As a result, the British, US and French decided that the German land they'd occupied since the end of the war should be united to create the Federal Republic of Germany (West Germany), and that their three remaining sectors of Berlin should become a part of it. This was finalized in May 1949. In October 1949, the USSR declared their occupied Germany territory to be the German Democratic Republic (East Germany) and East Berlin to be its capital city.

THE TWO BERLINS

For westerners to reach West Berlin, they had to travel through East Germany, or to fly over it, via agreed routes or 'corridors'. Life in capitalist West Berlin was much more relaxed than life in the communist East so, between 1949 and the drastic action that was to follow in 1961, 2.7 million – yes, that's 2,700,000 – fled from the Soviet-controlled East Germany to the West. More than half of these came via West Berlin. Eventually, the communist government ordered the building of a wall to surround the whole of West Berlin.

UP SPRINGS THE WALL

The wall came into being overnight on 13 August 1961. The original wall was not a true wall but was rolls of barbed wire, and the backs of people's houses (with the windows boarded and later bricked up). It was also lines of armed guards, who soon had their own watch towers to make sure than no one could escape. In those early days, though, people *did* escape. Families had been divided overnight and wanted to be together. Ways were found through cellars or other gaps in the defences until the proper wall was completed, with regular patrols and little hope of escape. The final 4-metre-high wall was 103 miles (166 kilometres) long, of which only 28 (45 kilometres) miles divided East Berlin from West. The rest of it separated West Berlin from the rest of East Germany. There were only twelve crossing points into West Berlin from East Germany, and only two crossing points between the East and West of the city, the most famous being Checkpoint Charlie.

SOVIET CLAIMS

The East Germans claimed that the Berlin Wall had been built to prevent any political or military interference from West Berlin and the West Germans, whilst it was clear to the West that it was really to keep the East Germans *in*! The East German government didn't want people getting to West Berlin via East Berlin or East Germany as a whole. In West Germany, it was possible to walk right up to the wall, and miles of it was covered in colourful graffiti. On the Eastern side, it was a different story. East Berliners couldn't get anywhere near the wall. There was an area of 'no man's land' along many of the stretches, with additional barbed-wire fencing, ditches and even tank traps to be crossed before anyone could get close to the actual Berlin Wall itself. That didn't stop people trying to escape

– many succeeded, but over a hundred were killed in the process.

THE GORBACHEV BROOM SWEEPS CLEAN

In 1985, a man named Mikhail Gorbachev became the General Secretary of the Communist Party in the USSR and, in 1988, President of the USSR itself. Unlike many Soviet leaders before him, he seemed genuinely interested in giving power and democratic rights to the people, rather than letting the top-heavy communist government keep a tight control on all aspects of Soviet life. He introduced two ideas to the USSR: *perestroika*, which is Russian for 'restructuring' and *glasnost* – 'openness'. He wanted to restructure the economy and to have openness in political and cultural life. He withdrew Soviet troops from disputed territories, signed arms treaties with old Cold War enemies, transferred power to legislatures elected by the people not run by the Communist Party, and gave Eastern bloc countries new freedoms.

THE END OF THE WALL

As a result of these incredible changes, in the summer of 1989, the former Eastern bloc Hungarians allowed East Germans to travel through Hungary if they wanted to get to Austria or West Germany. Power in East Germany was

crumbling. In one fell swoop, the Berlin Wall had become completely irrelevant. There was a much easier way out of East Germany than trying to cross into West Berlin! Come autumn, the former Soviet-backed East Germany government was teetering on the brink of collapse. Then, on 9 November 1989, the unthinkable happened: people started climbing up onto the Berlin Wall and knocking great chunks out of it – and nobody tried to stop them.

AFTER THE WALL

In the end, East Germany officially helped with the removal of the wall and, in 1990, the two countries were reunited as one: the Federal Republic of Germany, run along western lines. In the same year, Mikhail Gorbachev was awarded the Nobel Prize for Peace. In 1991, the USSR

– one of the most powerful empires in the twentieth century, if not history, collapsed and was no more. The world would never be the same again, and the fall of the Berlin Wall was a symbol of this incredible change.

THE FREEING OF
NELSON MANDELA

11 FEBRUARY 1990, NEAR VICTOR VERSTER PRISON,
SOUTH AFRICA

Crowds of reporters and photographers surge forward as a tall,
distinguished figure in a suit walks towards them along the
dusty road leading from the prison. Grey-haired, and even
slightly frail-looking, is this really the same man whose familiar,
younger face stares determinedly from posters across the globe?
Here, after almost 27 years in jail, is the first glimpse of Nelson
Mandela, free at last.

A MAN OF IDEALS

Nelson Mandela was
imprisoned in 1964 for
'sabotage and subversion'
against his home country of
South Africa. His real crime,
however, was being a black
person in a country where by
far the most people were
black, but were ruled by the
small minority of whites. Even
membership of the political party, the ANC (African
National Congress), which Nelson Mandela joined in

1944, had been made illegal in 1960 – the same year as the Sharpeville Massacre, in which around 70 black demonstrators were killed.

IN THE BEGINNING

Most white South Africans today are Afrikaners (sometimes called Boers), descended from settlers who originally came from the Netherlands. Britain wanted to rule South Africa, as part of its huge empire, but, in the late 1800s, some Afrikaners promoted the idea that they were 'the chosen people'. Britain defeated the Afrikaners in the First and Second Boer Wars, but two South African Afrikaner republics were granted self-rule by the British in 1907: the Transvaal and the Orange Free State. But soon the whole of South Africa was an independent country under Afrikaner rule. South Africa fought alongside Britain in the First World War, which upset many Afrikaners. In the Second World War, the loyalties of the Afrikaners were divided. Many supported Britain and the Allies, but many agreed with the anti-black ideas of Germany's Nazi Party. In 1948, the Afrikaner National Party, led by Daniel François Malan, won the election based on the issue of dividing whites from non-whites. Apartheid was born.

THE RISE OF THE NATIONALS

A year later, the National Party classed people as 'white', 'black', 'coloured' or 'Asian' and introduced the Group Areas Act. This law made sure that where you lived and worked, and what rights you had (or, more to the point, *didn't* have) depended on the colour of your skin. The whites ruled supreme, with the best houses, jobs and freedoms, and non-whites were treated like second- or third-class citizens. This became known as apartheid, from the Afrikaans language, meaning 'apart-hood'. But, in the 1990s, all this was about to change.

THE YOUNG MANDELA

Nelson Mandela, the son of a Xhosa-speaking chief, was born in 1918 in a village near Umtata, South Africa, in what is now Eastern Cape province. He went to the University of Fort Hare and quickly became a part of the political struggle against racial discrimination, and was kicked out in 1940 for his part in a student demonstration. He managed to finish his degree by taking a **correspondence course** with the University of South Africa and then went on to study for a law degree. He became more and more involved with the ANC – a nationalist movement made up of people of all skin colours – which hoped to bring about democratic change in South Africa.

A CAMPAIGN OF DEFIANCE

In 1952 the ANC launched the Defiance Campaign, in which protesters defied the apartheid laws across the whole of South Africa. Also in 1952, Nelson Mandela became one of the ANC's deputy presidents and national-Volunteer-in-Chief. Worried that the ANC would be banned, its leaders put something called the 'M' plan into operation. (The 'M' actually stood for Mandela!) The plan reorganized the ANC into small groups of members who could, in turn, encourage ordinary people to join the struggle against apartheid. The idea behind it was that a large number of small groups of volunteers would be much harder for government forces to **infiltrate** and put a stop to than one big, official organization. Mandela also opened up the first black law practice with his friend Oliver Tambo. Efforts to have him struck off the list of practising lawyers failed.

TAKING UP ARMS

As time went on, Mandela and others began to think that an armed struggle might be an important part of the fight against apartheid. Talking and demonstrating simply wasn't enough. In 1956, he found himself charged with treason, for his part in the various anti-apartheid, anti-government campaigns, at a trial which was to last five years. He was found innocent and acquitted.

MASSACRE!

In 1960 the ANC, along with another group called the PAC (Pan-Africanist Congress), called for a day of demonstrations on 21 March, right across the country, to protest against South Africa's pass laws. The pass laws strictly limited the movement and employment of black people, and meant that they had to carry their identity papers ('reference books') with them all the time. It was as a part of this day of demonstrations that a large crowd of

men, women and children gathered outside a police station in Sharpeville, Johannesburg. Some black people started burning their identity papers, some threw stones, and the (white) police opened fire. They kept on firing even when the terrified protesters started running away. Around 70 black men, women and children – figures vary from 67 to 72 – were killed and over 180 injured.

A STATE OF EMERGENCY

Uproar and outrage in the black community was immediate. There followed everything from peaceful protest marches and strikes to all-out riots, right across South Africa. A state of emergency was declared and over 18,000 people were arrested. The ANC and the PAC were banned, but continued in secret as illegal organizations. Countries around the world were horrified by what the South African government was doing, and South Africa's actions were officially condemned by the **United Nations**.

SPEAR OF THE NATION

Following the massacre, the now-banned ANC finally gave up their commitment to non-violence and a military wing, called 'Umkhonto we Sizwe' ('Spear of the Nation') was founded in December 1961, with Nelson Mandela as its commander-in-chief. Without getting official permission to leave the country – something all black people had to do – he went to the neighbouring country of Algeria for military training. When he returned to South Africa in 1962, he was arrested. At his trial, he conducted his own defence and began by saying, 'I detest racialism because I regard it as a barbaric thing, whether it comes from a black man or a white man.' He was sentenced to five years in prison.

SENTENCED TO LIFE

Soon, many of Nelson Mandela's ANC colleagues were arrested too, and he was put on trial alongside them for sabotage, treason and violent conspiracy. Found guilty, he was sentenced to life imprisonment in June 1964. For the next 18 years he was a prisoner in a tiny cell on Robben Island where conditions were very strict and harsh. Amazingly, Nelson Mandela and other political prisoners managed to keep in touch with apartheid groups secretly. He even managed to write most of his autobiography *Long Walk to Freedom* in captivity and to have it smuggled off Robben Island. Later, he was moved to another maximum-security prison, Pollsmoor Prison, near Cape Town. Finally, he was moved to Victor Verster Prison. Meanwhile, he'd become a symbol for the whole anti-apartheid movement, and world leaders and ordinary people protested for his release.

A NEW BEGINNING

It was as a result of this huge pressure, from home and abroad, that the then (white) president of South Africa, F. W. de Klerk, finally lifted the ban against the ANC and released Nelson Mandela in February 1990. After years of protest, de Klerk finally brought about a whites-only referendum in 1992, asking white people to back his plans to make a new constitution, giving proper rights to black people. Over two-thirds of the voters overwhelmingly voted for free elections for *everyone*. In 1993, both Mr de Klerk and Mr Mandela were awarded the Nobel Prize for Peace.

PRESIDENT MANDELA

In 1994, South Africa's first free elections brought the African Nation Congress to power, with Nelson Mandela as South Africa's first black president. 'Mr. Mandela has walked a long road and now stands at the top of the hill,' said F. W. de Klerk. Nelson Mandela himself described the election as: 'For all South Africa, an unforgettable occasion.' Nelson Mandela's release from prison was something that most people had thought was very unlikely. A black person being elected president of South Africa was an event that many people in the world had never dreamed was possible.

GLOSSARY

abdicate – to give up being the monarch

abolition – the act of abolishing or ending (in this case the slave trade or slavery)

air resistance – the force of the air resisting and slowing an object moving through it

aka – short for 'also known as'

amp – a unit of electricity (as in a 13 amp plug) used for measuring the amount of current required to produce a certain amount of force between two wires. Named after André Ampère

American Patriots – Colonists loyal to America, rather than Britain

archer – a soldier using a bow and arrow, longbow or crossbow

aviation – the science of building and flying aircraft

barbarians – the Roman name usually given to anyone living outside Roman territory

battery – a device which converts chemical energy into electrical energy, by means of a chemical reaction which produces a flow of electrons

beasts of burden – animals used to work (carry, plough, turn mill wheels etc.), often donkeys, asses, horses and oxen

Bronze Age – the first prehistoric humans used wood, bone and stone tools and this period was called the Stone Age. Later, they used bronze – a compound of copper and tin. This was the Bronze Age. It began in the Middle East in c.4500BC, but lasted in Britain from about 2000BC to 500BC. It was followed by the **Iron Age**

c. – short for the Latin word 'circa', meaning 'about'. A date marked *c.* means an approximate date; the event occurred around about then

capitalists – supporters of capitalism, an economic system based on the private ownership of capital (money, property, etc.)

census – an official account of all the people living in a country, made up from answers filled in questionnaires

classified – to say that a project is classified is shorthand for saying that it has been classified a secret by the government, probably for reasons of national security

coats-of-arms – design in the shape of a particular shield, representing a particular family

colonists – people setting up and living in a colony

colour blind – the inability to distinguish certain colours

colliery – a coal mine

Communists – members of, and believers in, a society where, in theory, everything belongs to the state and profits are shared amongst everyone

compounds – a substance made up of two or more chemical elements that can only be separated with a chemical reaction

conductor – material through which electricity flows freely

Confederate – a member of the breakaway Confederation of southern American states

conquistadors – sixteenth-century Spanish conquerors of the Americas

constitution – the stated rights of the people and the powers of their government

convex – bowing outwards

correspondence course – an educational course where student and teacher communicate by mail

cosmonaut – the Soviet name for

a space traveller (what the Americans call an astronaut)

Dark Ages – a period in European history from the late fifth century AD to about 1000 (a thousand years ago)

despotism – the rule of a tyrant

diaphragm – a thin disc that vibrates when receiving sound-waves, converting them into electrical signals, or which vibrates and produces sound-waves when turning electrical signals into sound

dog fights – close-up fights between two or more aeroplanes

element – a substance that cannot be split into simpler substances

empire – a group of countries with the same ruler, in this case Rome

employees – people working for someone. Edison's employees were employed by him. He paid their wages

facsimile – a very accurate copy

Fascists – followers of Fascism, a right-wing movement against democracy and liberalism, and for strict authority

farad – a unit of electrical capacity named after Faraday

flying shuttle – a device used in weaving for crossing the threads

forum – a place for open discussion

governor – Roman ruler of a foreign territory

gradual – over time (not straight away)

heresy – beliefs or statement going against the official rulings of the Church

hardware – the computer equipment itself, including the monitor, keyboard and hard disc, rather than the software

humidity – warmth and dampness

infiltrate – to secretly gain entry into

in theory – believed, but untried and untested

independently – on your own, without help from others

Iron Age – the period after the Bronze Age, involving the spread of iron weapons and tools, occurring at different times in different parts of the world

insulator – something which, in the case of an electrical insulator, stops electricity passing through it

intercontinental ballistic missile – a missile with a nuclear warhead that can travel over 5,500 km

Kaiser – German Emperor

low church – Christians who were against statues and finery, believing in humility (being humble) and simplicity

low-resistance – an easy route for electricity, down a high conductor (resistance is the opposition of flow to an electric current)

Loyalists – those American colonists loyal to Britain

lift – gravity is the force that tries to keep everything (including aeroplanes) firmly on the ground. Lift is the upward force which overcomes gravity, keeping planes in the sky. Lift is produced by wings and propeller blades with a special aerofoil shape moving through the air. (Looking at it from the side, an aerofoil wing or propeller blade has a larger curve on its upper surface than its lower surface)

literate – able to read and write

lithographic plates – printing plates where certain areas (in the shapes of the letters) are made ink-receptive, whilst the surrounding areas remain ink-repellent

mass – the amount of physical matter an object contains, nowadays usually measured in grams

masses – the mass population. Lots of us lot!

mass-produced – goods manufactured in large numbers to the same design

Mediterranean area – countries bordering the Mediterranean Sea, a large inland sea between South Europe, North Africa and South-west Asia

mercury – sometimes called quicksilver, a liquid metal often found in thermometers

misconception – a commonly held belief that isn't actually true

molecule – usually two or more atoms bonded together

mutinies – revolts against those in charge (often regular troops rising up against officers)

naval blockade – tactic preventing ships or supplies getting in or out

Nazis – members of the **fascist** National Socialist German Worker's Party, with racist and brutal ideals

Nazism – beliefs of the Nazi party (led by Adolf Hitler)

newsreel – news captured on film and shown in a weekly news round-up at the cinema, in the days before television was so popular

Nobel Prize – an annual prize given to outstanding contributions to physics, chemistry, physiology, medicine, literature, peace, and now economics too. Awarded by an international committee in Sweden (except for the peace prize, awarded in Norway)

nuclear fallout – side effects, secondary consequences of a nuclear explosion

nucleus *plural:* **nuclei** – the heart of an atom, made up of protons and neutrons

neutrality – the not taking of sides

nutritious – full of nutrients, which your body can use to keep you strong and healthy

obsolete – outdated, outmoded, yesterday's model

offensive – attacking (rather than defensive)

Official Secrets Act – a British law designed to prevent people from giving away important government secrets

offspring – a plant's, animal's or human's 'child'

optical – using light

parachute – a large piece of cloth, attached to a person by thin ropes, designed to open out in a canopy, slow down the person – who has jumped or been ejected from a plane – and bring him or her safely to the ground

papyrus – paper made from a fibrous plant

patent – a legal permit designed to stop others stealing your invention. A patent prevents everyone else from making or selling the invention you have patented

patron – a benefactor or someone who sponsors another to do some work, e.g. research, painting

pedestrians – people going around on foot

phenomena *single:* **phenomenon** – occurrences

philanthropists – people, usually wealthy, who perform charitable and benevolent acts to help others

phonic alphabet – an alphabet in which the letters go together to create written versions of the sounds required to say words

Pony Express – a mail delivery service in the American West, using relays of horse and riders.

It was at its height from Missouri to California in 1860–61, and surprisingly fast

persevere – to stick at doing something

projectiles – any objects fired from a gun. These could be large iron balls, tiny lead pellets and, later, bullets and shells

propeller – a series of blades, shaped like small aerofoil wings on their sides. A propeller creates lift, sucking itself (and the aeroplane) along – propelling the plane forwards – pushing out air behind it

province – an area outside Rome itself, but controlled by Romans

punctuation – symbols (not letters) used to divide up sentences, showing who's speaking, for example, when writing

Quakers – members of the Society of Friends. Christians who reject rituals and at whose religious meetings anyone can speak

qwerty – a 'qwerty' keyboard is a standard English keyboard with the top line of letters beginning with the letters 'q', 'w', 'e', 'r', 't' and 'y'

Renaissance – flowering of the arts in Europe, from the fourteenth to sixteenth centuries, inspired by the works of the Ancient Romans and Greeks

republic – a country or state which elects its government and which doesn't have a king, queen or emperor

revolution – one complete turn of a circle. 'Revolutions per minute' are the number of times an object completes a revolution in a minute

rotors – the rotating blades of a helicopter, fixed to a central stem. The rotors produce the thrust and lift to make the machine fly

sap – the liquid in trees and plants. Tree sap often hardens into a goo

satellites – machines orbiting the Earth (often receiving signals from and sending signals to satellite dishes on Earth)

senators – members of the Senate, Rome's governing council

side effects – effects in addition to those actually intended (for example, the side effect of loud music might be a headache, or ringing in the ears)

signet – a seal used to stamp documents, often set in a (signet) ring

silicon chips – sometimes called microchips; tiny pieces of silicon with electronic circuits printed on them

software – computer programs and operating systems, rather than the actual hardware

Soviets – people of the USSR

sprocket – a wheel with 'teeth' on either rim, designed to catch in holes down the side of a strip of film to pull it through the camera or projector

stylus – a pointed instrument. Later, a stylus came to mean the needle of a record player, often tipped with a diamond

sovereign – a king or queen

Soviet – someone from the Soviet Union, a communist federal republic in Eastern Europe and North Asia led by Russia and known as the USSR. Disbanded in 1991

spectrum – the full range of colours making up white light: red, orange, yellow, blue, green, indigo, violet

subatomic – smaller than an atom. Subatomic particles include electrons, protons and neutrons

synthetic – human-made or artificial

transported – taken abroad to a penal colony

364

thermosetting plastics – types of plastics which don't melt when heated. Thermo- plastics are the plastics that do

trenches – a system of large ditches used to protect troops at the front line

Tsar – the Emperor of Russia

unifier – someone who 'unifies', brings people together

Unionist – an American loyal to the United States of America and against the breakaway Confederation in the south

United Nations – an association of states pledged to world peace and security, working throughout the world through such organizations as the World Health Organization (WHO) and the United Nations Children's Fund (UNICEF). The UN's security council is responsible for sending UN troops (drawn from different member states) to police 'hot spots' across the globe

USSR – the Union for Soviet Socialist Republics, or Soviet Union, made up of a variety of communist republics, including Russia (no longer exists)

vacuum – a place without gas or air, as in space

valves – vacuum devices used to control a flow of electrons in electric circuits

vapour – a gas, usually one that's been changed from a liquid or a solid

vibration – the act of something vibrating (rapidly moving back and forth, quivering)

virus – an organism that multiplies in the body's cells, often causing disease

volt – a unit for measuring the electrical potential between two points – the work that has to be done to move a unit of positive charge from one point to another. Named after Alessandro Volta

watt – a unit of electrical power (as in 60 watt bulb)

Index